CHAMP THORNTON

RADICALLY
DIFFERENT

TEACHER GUIDE

A STUDENT'S GUIDE TO COMMUNITY

CHAMP THORNTON

RADICALLY DIFFERENT

A STUDENT'S GUIDE TO COMMUNITY

TEACHER GUIDE

New Growth Press, Greensboro, NC 27404
www.newgrowthpress.com
Copyright © 2019 by Champ Thornton

Cover Design: Faceout Books, faceoutstudio.com
Interior Design, Illustration, and Typesetting: Scot McDonald

ISBN 978-1-645070-32-0 (Print)
ISBN 978-1-64507-055-9 (eBook)

Printed in the United States of America
26 25 24 23 22 21 20 19   1 2 3 4 5

Contents

A Word For Teachers and Parents

For years my wife and I have said that we want our three children to grow up and leave our home "in sync with reality." What we mean is that we want them to be in touch with the realities that exist in God's universe.

For starters, there is a loving and holy God; he's made a very good world, yet it's also broken now because of human sin. Yet God, in his love, sent his Son to rescue us and, who, one day, will set everything right once again. We want our children to live in a way that reflects this "true story of the whole world."[1]

Yet society around us and our desires within us tell a different story—starring video games, cool apps, social media, friends, sports, movies, music, and fashion. In this version of life, out of sync with reality, God is absent, sin is renamed, and the Rescuer is irrelevant.

To get an accurate picture of life in this world, we must simultaneously view all of life through three lenses. The first lens provides the view that originally God made everything very *good* (Genesis 1). The next lens reveals that this good world is now also *bad*, broken and tainted by sin (Genesis 3). The third clarifies that Jesus came to make *new* everything that was broken by sin (Romans 8). Creation, Fall, Redemption—good, bad, new.[2]

If you leave out any of these lenses, you will neglect some aspect of reality that God intends for us and our children to embrace. So on week one, we start with God—always the best place to start any study of Scripture. The next three weeks look at what the Bible says about each "lens." The remainder of the study considers one new topic—featuring relationships—each week, using this three-part lens.

Radically Different doesn't aim to be exhaustive or provide a topical dictionary of issues, but to help middle-school students begin to think biblically about life and relationships. Through your ministry, may the Lord lead their relationships to be radically biblical and *radically different.*

How to Use This Teacher Guide

The Book at a Glance

The first four weeks of *Radically Different* set the groundwork for the remainder of the book. Week 1 begins with what is most important—God himself. Weeks 2–4 introduce the three lenses through which to look at every question. They are the following:

Week 2: Creation (*good*—God made everything "very good")
Week 3: Fall (*bad*—everything is messed up because of sin)
Week 4: Redemption (*new*—God sent Jesus to set things right)

In other words, when trying to figure something out, in relationships or anywhere else in life, ask these three questions:

- How is it good because God made it (Creation)?
- How is it messed up because of Adam and Eve's sin (the Fall)?
- And how has Jesus's death restored it to its original goodness—or even better (Redemption)?

CREATION	FALL	REDEMPTION
God made it . . .	We broke it . . .	Jesus fixes it.[3]
Good	Bad	New
God's World Designed	God's World Bent	God's World Restored

These three words—good, bad, new—are like three lenses of a telescope. Look at everything in life through all three lenses.

The Weekly Plan

When you get together with your students each week, they should have already worked their way through the week's material in their student book.

Here's an overview of the elements in your Teacher Guide and what your time with your students might look like each week:

Content Overview. This paragraph provides you with a summary of what your students are learning each week. Leaders could use this paragraph to give a quick orientation to parents or discussion leaders.

Aims. These objectives capture the point of each Day from that week in the Student Guide.

Getting Started (5–10 minutes). Use the Story Starter or Icebreaker Idea to broadly introduce the topic you'll be discussing. Also, if your group is large enough, you may want to keep the entire group together for the introduction before splitting up into smaller discussion groups for the remainder of the time.

Memorize (10–15 minutes). Add this element at the beginning or end of your lesson. Scripture memorization is about treasuring God's Word. Students will work to memorize Colossians 3:1–4:1, which features many aspects of Christian relationships. Encourage students to spend time at home memorizing the week's passage.

Discussion Questions (15–20 minutes). As you lead the group through the week's material, encourage discussion by asking some of the suggested questions at appropriate times. Some additional teaching notes are also included.

Next Steps (10–15 minutes). The aim of this section is to help the students have a clear action plan for living out what they've learned. You may find that students have other, even better, ideas for how to apply the text to life.

This pre-lesson will introduce *Radically Different* to your group. Distribute the books and walk the group through the organization of the first lesson so they can see what is expected of them each week.

Take a few minutes to introduce students to the passage they'll be memorizing over the course of this study: Colossians 3:1–4:1. Students may memorize from any Bible version you prefer.

GETTING STARTED
Option 1. Story Starter
Tell a story about a time when you saw the stars and they seemed especially brilliant—perhaps on a camping trip or through a telescope. Explain why the stars were so clear and vivid and relate what kind of impact that experience had on you.

Option 2. Icebreaker Idea
Use a packing tube or sleeve of a rain jacket to serve as a "telescope." Tell your group that you're going to do some stargazing, using this telescope. Ask for volunteers to look through the telescope.

Ask for three volunteers, and tell each person to identify what objects they see through the telescope. Have the first volunteer look through one end of the telescope, as you pass a Mars candy bar past the other end. For the second volunteer, you can use a Milky Way candy bar. For the third volunteer, you announce that it's the Big Dipper as you pass a Styrofoam cup (with some water in it and with "the Big Dipper" written on the side) past the other end, and pour the contents down the telescope.

Often, a telescope will have more than one lens for magnification. Like a telescope, God's Word also provides more than one lens for looking at life. God has given us his Word to help us not only learn about him, but also learn about life—and that includes relationships.

INTRODUCE *RADICALLY DIFFERENT*
Distribute copies of the *Radically Different* student guide. Have the group open their books and show them the Contents page. Read through the introductory material together.

Explain that the first four weeks will be an introduction to the entire study, giving attention to the following topics, one per week: God, Good (creation), Bad (fall), and New (redemption).

The remaining weeks will cover one topic per week within the overarching category of community or relationships, whether with God or with other people. During a typical week, students will look at the topics through three lenses. Day one will use the "good" lens, day two the "bad" lens, and day three the "new" lens.

NEXT STEPS
Have leaders share how they have grown and changed in the area of their time with the Lord (prayer, Bible reading, etc.). Ask students what practices they have found most helpful in this aspect of their lives. Encourage all students to make plan for their time in the Word and prayer this week.

CONTENT OVERVIEW

Students will learn that Jesus is always revealing what God the Father is like. For example, Christ reveals that God is love, and this love is an essential aspect of God in his tri-unity ("the Trinity"). The Father, Son, and Spirit have always loved the other members of the Godhead. It is in God's very nature to show love to others, and it's his own love that he pours out on his people.

Aims
• To encourage students in the love of God that he loves to show
• To clarify that Jesus exactly reflects the Father
• To introduce the doctrine of the Trinity

Memorize
Colossians 3:1–2

GETTING STARTED
Option 1. Story Starter
Tell a story about how people have said you are like one of your parents.

Option 2. Icebreaker Idea
Ask one of your students to draw a caricature of you, the teacher.

Ask the group what part of the drawing looks most like you. (Discuss.)

When you draw caricatures, the key is to take a few unique characteristics and exaggerate them.

Read John 1:14. When the Bible says that Jesus fully reveals what the Father is like—in contrast to caricatures—what aspects or characteristics of the Father do you think he is displaying? (Discuss.) You can also look up and discuss Hebrews 1:1–3.

It's easy to think that Jesus showed us the Father when he calmed a storm or raised the dead. But the Bible teaches that Jesus is the exact image of the Father. Every word, every act of kindness, every miracle, and every instance of self-sacrifice revealed the Father. If you want to know what God is like, then look at Jesus in the Bible.

WEEK ONE
GOD

This book is about relationships. But where to start? There are so many different people in your life—friends and family members, people at school and at church, fun people and not-so-fun people. Where do we dive in? Let's start where it's always best to begin—with God himself.

The Bible helps you see him, like a telescope helps you look at stars. When you look at a star—massive and erupting with energy—*without* a telescope, it seems like a tiny twinkle in the night sky. In the same way, some people imagine God as a distant and kind, bearded old man. Yet if you could really see what God is like, you'd be blown away! He's ablaze with limitless power, wisdom, beauty, and love. And this is how the Bible helps us see what God is truly like.

So when you open God's Word, remember to always look for who God is and what he's like. But before you start to read the passage of Scripture for each day this week, take time to pray from your heart this prayer or one like it.

PRAYER

"God, you have told us what you're like in your Word; please help me to really see what you've written, and most of all to see and get to know you better. In Jesus's name, Amen."

("Amen," means something like, "this is what I really mean," or "let it be so," or "I agree with what I've said." But most people usually just mean: "I'm done praying now.")

Day 1

Read John 1:14 and 18 (below). Remember, ask the Lord to help you understand what you've read.

> ¹⁴ And the Word became flesh and dwelt among us, and we have seen his glory, glory as of the only Son from the Father, full of grace and truth. . . . ¹⁸ No one has ever seen God; the only God, who is at the Father's side, he has made him known. John 1:14, 18

▶ In John 1:14, someone is given the title "the Word." Whoever this is, he's communicating a very important message from God. Who do you think this is? (Hint: In the Bible who became human and lived among other human beings?)

Jesus Christ

▶ According to these verses, where can people see God? Who has made him known? Put verse 18 in your own words.

(When you see a lowercase letter after a verse number, that indicates a certain part of the verse. So, for example: verse "18a," refers to the first part of verse 18, usually up to the first punctuation mark, like a comma or semicolon. Verse 18b, would refer to the next section, and 18c would be the third section, etc.)

God the Father has made the Son known; see John 1:18.

THINK ABOUT IT

If you want to see what God is like, look at Jesus. You can see what God is like in the powerful ways Jesus healed people, defeated demons, and controlled the weather. But as God's Son, Jesus revealed the Father in *everything* he did. Every kind word, every humble act of service, every moment of patience—all this shows you what our God is truly like in real-life ways we can understand.

Jesus revealed the Father in *everything* he did.

Day 2

Read 1 John 4:8 (below). (After you read, take time to pray the prayer at the beginning of this week, and then read 1 John 4:8 again.)

> { ⁸ Anyone who does not love does not know God, because God is love. 1 John 4:8

○ On Day 1, you learned how Jesus showed us exactly what God the Father is like. He revealed him. The question for today is what did Jesus reveal about the Father? What does 1 John 4:8 say that God is?

> *God is love.*

○ Which of the following does this verse NOT say? Cross through the wrong answers.

- • ~~God "does loving things."~~
- • ~~God "became love" by sending Jesus.~~
- • ~~God is "usually loving."~~
- • God is love.

○ What do you think it means when John wrote, God is love?

> *God in his deepest person—who he "is"—is a God of love.*

○ Did you realize that God, at his very heart, *loves to love?* That's what he is actually like—at his core.

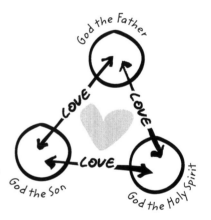

All this can be hard to think about. But here is the basic point: there has never, ever been a time when God was not full and overflowing with love. God *is* love. Take a moment and ask God to pour out his love into your heart today.

Day 3

So far this week, we've seen that Jesus shows us exactly what God is like, and what we learn about God is that he is full of love. That's just what he's like; no one twists his arm to be loving.

▶ But if God is love (not that he "became" love), what did God love *before* he created everything? Give this some thought, then write down your ideas.

> God the Father loved the Son and Spirit, the Son loved the Father and Spirit, and the Spirit loved the Father and Son.

Read John 17:24.

> 24 Father, I desire that they also, whom you have given me, may be with me where I am, to see my glory that you have given me because you loved me before the foundation of the world. John 17:24

▶ How does this verse answer the previous question? What was God doing before he made the universe? Whom was he loving?

> The Father has always loved his Son.

THINK ABOUT IT

This will not fit into our little human brains, but here's the mind-blowing truth: God has always been. And what he's always been is this: a loving Father to his Son. God the Father has always loved the Son, and the Son has always loved the Father (John 14:31). Together with the Holy Spirit, the Father and Son didn't make the world and people because they needed someone to love (they had each other, right?). Instead, because they were already so full of love—and always had been—the Father, Son, and Spirit created the world to share their love with others.

IN CLOSING

IT'S NOT ROCKET SCIENCE

If you've been around other Christians, you've probably heard the term "Trinity." This term is a compound word:

"tri" (three) + "[u]nity."

It refers to the fact that in the Bible there is one God in three persons: Father, Son, and Spirit. This seems impossible to figure out. But the Trinity is not an addition problem in math; it's not a formula in science.

Instead, the Tri-unity of God means that at his very core, God is *relational*. The Father has always loved the Son and Spirit. The Son and Spirit have always loved the Father and each other (John 14:31; 16:14–15; 17:24). It's in God's deepest nature to love and show love to others (Hosea 11:9). And he's always been that way. C. S. Lewis, author of the Chronicles of Narnia said it this way:

❝In Christianity God is not a static thing—not even a person—but a dynamic, pulsating activity, a life, almost a kind of drama. Almost, if you will not think me irreverent, a kind of dance.... [The] pattern of this three-Personal life is . . . a great fountain of energy and beauty spurting up at the very centre of reality.❞ 4

So, for Christians, when God says he loves you, he means it from the bottom of his heart. When you ask him to show compassion or mercy, you don't have to convince him or try to make him do something he doesn't want to do. The Tri-unity of God means that he is—and always has been—full and overflowing with love.

1. What stood out to you from the Word this week? (How has the Lord been using his Word to work in your life this week?)

2. Who here has ever actually looked through a telescope or microscope? What did you notice that you hadn't seen before?

3. What do we learn about God when we look at Jesus? (see John 1:14)

4. How are these two statements different: "God is loving" and "God is love"?

5. Which would you want to be true about another person in your life (a parent, friend, etc.)—that _____ is loving or that _____ is love? Why?

6. Challenge Question. Imagine a different situation. What if, in a made-up world, there was a God who did not really like to love? In this situation, love would not be in his very nature. How would you feel if this kind of God said he would forgive you when you disobey? How would you feel if this kind of God said you were now his child in his family?

7. Based on what you read this week, what are some wrong answers to the question, Why did God create people?

8. If God "is love," how do you think God thinks about you when you've sinned or messed up?

9. If God "is love" at his core, then how should you feel when you've asked him to forgive you?

Next Steps
Your students' love should reflect God's love. Brainstorm with them about some ways they can show real love to others. This is not about coming across as nice people, rather it's about having (and demonstrating) real love for others. Encourage your students to write down two ways they can show God's love to others this week.

Teacher Guide

Week Two: Good

CONTENT OVERVIEW
In the beginning God created the world, and he created it all very good. God made human beings to resemble and represent him on earth. As such they were to both enjoy and take care of the good world he had made. And part of his very good world were the rules he gave for people to obey.

Aims
- To remind your students that we are all on planet Earth to resemble and represent our Creator
- To help students feel their responsibility to not only enjoy what God has made, but also take care of it (as cultivators, not merely consumers)
- To show that even God's rules were made good

Memorize
Colossians 3:3–4

GETTING STARTED
Option 1. Story Starter
Tell a story about a time when you didn't adequately take care of something that belonged to you.

Option 2. Icebreaker Idea
This week we've been looking at the "goodness" of the world God created. And for many people that wouldn't exclude the goodness of bacon.

Show this bacon pie chart to the group (http://cdn.foodbeast.com/content/uploads/2014/05/bacon-pie-chart.jpg). You could, alternatively, bring in a warm plate of bacon!

What is your favorite recipe using this most essential food group?

Now, if you're not a bacon fan, let's move to a different topic. What things that God has made come to mind right away as "good"?

GREAT TO MEET YOU DUDE...

WEEK TWO
GOOD

CHALLENGE
Open your Bible to Genesis 1 and count how many times God said what he made was good.

(Seven times—Genesis 1:4, 10, 12, 18, 21, 25, 31)

The Bible begins with the story of how God made the world. Again and again, he sized up what he'd made, and he said it was "good."

All of it was "very good" (Genesis 1:31)! The whole created universe was top quality. No defects, no flaws, nothing to displease or disappoint.

What made it all so fantastic? The answer is that everything, like a mirror, reflected what God himself is like (Psalm 19:1). God made the universe for the loving reason of showing people how amazing he is, how beautiful, and how kind!

What's your favorite song? Whatever it is, could you imagine getting to meet the artist who wrote it or sings it? Forever after, whenever you heard the song, you would always think of the artist.

This is *why* God created. He made everything good to remind us of him! But here's a new question to think about this week: If we're part of God's very good creation, *how* does he want us to live? (Before you answer, take a moment to talk to the Lord.)

PRAYER

"Father, you are the creator and sustainer of the universe. Thank you for making everything and for making it all so good. Help me give thanks to you through the day for all the things I enjoy. They all come from your good heart. And as I enjoy the creation, help me to enjoy you even more. In Jesus's name, Amen."

Day 1

This week we're looking at the *goodness* of creation. Read the first part of Genesis 1:26.

> Then God said, "Let us make man in our image, after our likeness." Genesis 1:26a

▶ According to what design did God craft man and woman?

According to God's own image and likeness

THINK ABOUT IT

Made in God's image, every person has dignity and value. All creation reflects its Creator in some way. But humans were designed to resemble God in a special way. The portrait of a president hanging in a government building looks like the president, but it also represents the president's authority in that location. In the same way, God has put his representatives all over the earth. Men and women were created to represent and resemble their Creator.

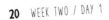

Now read the second part of Genesis 1:26.

> [God said:] "And let [the man and the woman] have dominion over the fish of the sea and over the birds of the heavens and over the livestock and over all the earth and over every creeping thing that creeps on the earth." Genesis 1:26b

▶ As God's representatives, what are humans supposed to do on earth?

> Rule over—that is, take care of—the entire world God has made.

▶ Read Genesis 2:15 (below). Circle the words that show other ways that humans represent God through their actions.

> The LORD God took the man and put him in the garden of Eden to work it and keep it. Genesis 2:15

Being made "in the image of God" teaches that we, like him, should **creatively cultivate** the world around us. List three areas that you can protect and develop, as you're encouraged to do in Genesis 1:26b and 2:15. Following are several items listed to get you started:

▶ I can cultivate my part of God's good world by

* making my room more orderly and attractive.
* helping with dishes and laundry.
* organizing my homework (or helping someone who might be struggling in this area).

Day 2

God made everything good. Read Genesis 2:16–17 (below). In these verses, what is the first command God gave?

"You may surely eat of every tree of the garden."

{ ¹⁶ And the Lᴏʀᴅ God commanded the man, saying, "You may surely eat of every tree of the garden, ¹⁷ but of the tree of the knowledge of good and evil you shall not eat, for in the day that you eat of it you shall surely die." Genesis 2:16–17

◐ According to 1 Timothy 6:17 (below), why did God give us everything he's created?

So that we could enjoy what he had made.

◐ Everything God made is good and to be enjoyed. If God wants you to enjoy what he's created, how does that change your thoughts about what God is like?

{ As for the rich in this present age, charge them not to be haughty, nor to set their hopes on the uncertainty of riches, but on God, who richly provides us with everything to enjoy. 1 Timothy 6:17

Day 3

- Everything God created is good. Reread Genesis 2:16–17. In your own words, what does God command in verse 17?

> *Do not eat from the tree of the knowledge of good and evil.*

- If everything God had created was good, why do you think God even gave rules to be obeyed?

> *Because God's rules were also pointing the way toward what was good. God's rules were good too.*

Part of the goodness of creation is that God designed it to be enjoyed and cultivated within boundaries. In creation, as in board games, there are "rules of play" that make life fun and good. Many of these rules of play are commanded by God in the Bible. They tell us how life works best. For examples of these very good rules which relate to relationships, read Exodus 20:12–17.

> "¹²Honor your father and your mother, that your days may be long in the land that the LORD your God is giving you. ¹³You shall not murder. ¹⁴You shall not commit adultery. ¹⁵You shall not steal. ¹⁶You shall not bear false witness against your neighbor. ¹⁷You shall not covet your neighbor's house; you shall not covet your neighbor's wife, or his male servant, or his female servant, or his ox, or his donkey, or anything that is your neighbor's." Exodus 20:12–17

THINK ABOUT IT

Did you know that these rules of play aren't just written in words? God's rules are hardwired into creation itself. God created an order or structure in life that you can't escape. For example, isn't lying or murdering considered wrong by most people in most cultures? Selfless friendships are appreciated by almost everyone, right? And don't you agree that people need to love and be loved by others? God designed his world, even though it's broken by sin, to operate according to his rules of play.

▶ Read Deuteronomy 10:13 (below). And then rephrase it in your own words.

{ "[God requires you] to keep the commandments and statutes of the LORD, which I am commanding you today for your good."
Deuteronomy 10:13

▶ Are there any of God's rules of play that you find difficult to keep? Pause to talk to the Lord about your struggle.

IN CLOSING

a REAL PaNE

Did you know that you can look at everything in this world just like you look at a window? You can look at something or you can look *through* something.

At least this is what a pastor named George Herbert thought. Born in Wales (which borders England) in 1593, he only lived 39 years. But what a full life!

As a young man, he first served in the royal court of the British king, James I. He wrote speeches for the king. After a few years, George believed God was calling him to be a pastor. Now he would speak for another King. God had given him a talent with words. At heart, George was a poet.

Whatever God was teaching him, George tried to express it by writing poetry. George Herbert knew that God had created everything. So to George, enjoying what God had made without seeing the God who made it was like looking *at* a window, but not looking *through* it. George said it like this:

Teach me, my God and King,
In all things Thee to see,
And what I do in anything,
To do it as for Thee.

A man who looks on glass,
On it may fix his sight,
Or, if he pleases, through it pass,
To view the heavens bright.[5]

In other words, you can look at your abilities in sports, or you can look *through* them. You can look at your dinner, or look through it. At your tech devices, or through them. At your relationships, or through them.

What lies beyond everything that you enjoy? God himself. The Creator. He made everything for your enjoyment and for his praise. So don't just look at life. Look *through* it, see the Creator, and give him thanks.

1. What stood out to you from the Word this week? (How has the Lord been using his Word to work in your life this week?)

2. What favorite gift have you received, and who was it from? When you enjoy(ed) this gift, did it remind you of the person who gave it to you? In what way?

3. What does God want his representatives on earth to do? What are our responsibilities as his representatives?

4. Of all the things God has made, what does God want us to enjoy? What do you enjoy most? Is this a good thing?

5. What is the difference between merely consuming something and cultivating something? Which is better? Which would you rather do? Why?

6. Why do you think God would give rules anyway? If he could make any world he wanted, why make one with rules? What do you think?

7. Let's imagine that you took time to create a board game for your family or friends. What do you hope they will get out of the game? How do you hope they will think about the rules of play? What might they do with the rules of play that would disappoint you? Why?

8. How do your friends tend to view rules? Why?

9. If God's rules are good, what's good about them?

Next Steps

Divide your group into smaller groups of two to three. Have each group come up with a plan for both enjoying and also cultivating some part of God's good creation this week. Two guidelines for their project are: (1) the plan must honor the Bible's boundaries, and (2) the plan should remind people in the group or outside the group about how good God himself is. (Ideas could include conservation activities, cleaning and organizing areas in need of help, etc.)

CONTENT OVERVIEW
This week examines the Fall, when the first humans sinned after being tempted by Satan. This temptation falsely called into question the goodness of the Creator, and it also valued the goodness of creation far above its proper place. Sin values what God has made too highly, instead of supremely valuing the God who made it. Lastly, Adam and Eve soon felt the consequences of their sin, which affected and tainted—without completely ruining—every aspect of life.

Aims
• To show how temptation calls into question God's goodness
• To introduce the concept of idolatry (i.e., valuing a created thing too highly, in the place reserved for only God)
• To remind how sin has truly affected everything in life, bending all things away from their original goodness

Memorize
Colossians 3:5–6

GETTING STARTED
Option 1. Story Starter
Share a story about how the Lord confronted you with your sinfulness—how he brought a sin to your attention.

Option 2. Icebreaker Idea
A lot of stuff gets broken in life, when it shouldn't be broken. If you could snap your fingers and fix a problem with the world today, what would you fix?

There's a famous story about the British religious author, G. K. Chesterton, who lived from 1874–1936. Supposedly, a London newspaper, *The Times*, asked their readership, "What is wrong with the world today?" Chesterton, known for his quick mind and sharp pen, wrote back:

> Dear Sir,
>
> I am.
>
> Yours,
>
> G. K. Chesterton

WEEK THREE
BAD

Remember how Genesis 1 and 2 explain that God created the world good? Well, in the very next chapter of Genesis, the story jumps from good to bad.

This "badness" doesn't mean destroyed, like when a big car wreck means your vehicle is totaled and headed for the junkyard. Instead, it means that everything God made has been twisted and corrupted—bent out of its original shape.

Nothing on earth escapes this damage. Mankind's relationship with God is broken. Our relationships with other people are broken. Our relationship with this world is broken. And our relationship to our own self is broken. Every single good thing, all that God had made, is warped—bent—by this badness.

Did You Know?

Bible teachers call the cause of this badness the "Fall" because it's the story of how the first humans (Adam and Eve) fell from their original goodness. At the start they had been good and righteous and holy, but then came the Fall.

What happened? That's what we'll look at this week. Here's a prayer to get you started:

PRAYER

"Lord, you are the giver of all good rules. How kind of you to tell us how life is best lived. Please forgive me for living as my own boss, making and obeying my own laws. Help me really believe that your ways are good and best. In Jesus's name. Amen."

Day 1

The badness begins. Read Genesis 3:1.

> Now the serpent was more crafty than any other beast of the field that the LORD God had made. He said to the woman, "Did God actually say, 'You shall not eat of any tree in the garden'?" Genesis 3:1

○ In this verse Satan, who was disguised as a snake, asks Eve a question. Write down his question word-for-word as it appears in your Bible.

○ Compare Genesis 3:1 with Genesis 2:16–17 (see Week 2, Day 2). What had God *actually* said? Explain how Satan twisted God's actual statement.

> *God had said they should not eat from one tree, but should eat from all the others. Satan accused God of saying they couldn't eat from any of the trees in the garden.*

○ Circle the aspect of God's character that Satan was attacking:

Justice   Forgiveness

Holiness   Majesty

(Goodness)

▶ In your own words, describe how Satan wanted God to appear in the minds of Adam and Eve.

> Satan wanted God to appear not good and not generous, but instead to seem stingy and harsh.

▶ List five things you really, really want badly. (To get you started, this could be a friendship. Or is it a skill? An app or game?) Think and pray about how you might be missing the goodness of what you *already have* been given by God. (Hint: These blessings might include family, forgiveness, second chances, love, acceptance, etc.)

Day 2

Let's continue to look at the bad that has bent God's good world. Read Genesis 3:4–6.

> [4] But the serpent said to the woman, "You will not surely die. [5] For God knows that when you eat of it your eyes will be opened, and you will be like God, knowing good and evil." [6] So when the woman saw that the tree was good for food, and that it was a delight to the eyes, and that the tree was to be desired to make one wise, she took of its fruit and ate, and she also gave some to her husband who was with her, and he ate. Genesis 3:4–6

▶ From these verses, use your own words to describe what three things attracted Eve to the fruit that God had forbidden.

> *The fruit seemed delicious; it looked beautiful; and it had been promised (by Satan) to fill the eater with wisdom.*

▶ At the moment of her temptation, what did Eve value most? What did she no longer value?

> *Eve valued what the fruit could do for her—the benefits it seemed to offer to her. She also valued the words of the serpent more than the words of God.*

By eating the very appealing fruit, Eve chose to worship something instead of God. This kind of God-substitute is what the Bible calls an "idol." *Idolatry* is when you treat something God made (something good) as too important (more important than God).

THINK ABOUT IT

A stone is a thing created by God, but when it's carved into a statue and people pray to it like a god, it becomes an idol. It's something that's created that's being treated like it's the Creator. And to this day, sin—at its heart—is loving something God has given more than loving the God who gave it.

Here's an example: When you love something like sports or friendship so much that you're willing to lie just a little bit in order to make everything work out the way you want, what is going on? You are loving the good thing (sports, friendship) more than God, who commands us to tell the truth.

▶ Is there anything that you love too much? Think about things you like to do. Or things you own—or *want* to own. Pick one thing which you're starting to realize that you love too much. In your own words, describe how you can tell that it's too important to you.

Day 3

Today our study of badness continues. Read Genesis 3:7–13 (below). Circle everything in this passage that was affected by Adam and Eve's sin.

⁷ Then the eyes of both were opened, and they knew that they were naked. And they sewed fig leaves together and made themselves loincloths. ⁸ And they heard the sound of the Lᴏʀᴅ God walking in the garden in the cool of the day, and the man and his wife hid themselves from the presence of the Lᴏʀᴅ God among the trees of the garden. ⁹ But the Lᴏʀᴅ God called to the man and said to him, "Where are you?" ¹⁰ And he said, "I heard the sound of you in the garden, and I was afraid, because I was naked, and I hid myself." ¹¹ He said, "Who told you that you were naked? Have you eaten of the tree of which I commanded you not to eat?" ¹² The man said, "The woman whom you gave to be with me, she gave me fruit of the tree, and I ate." ¹³ Then the Lᴏʀᴅ God said to the woman, "What is this that you have done?" The woman said, "The serpent deceived me, and I ate."
Genesis 3:7–13

▶ **Your relationship with yourself.** How did sin affect what Adam and Eve thought about themselves? How did they feel inside after sinning? What does Genesis 3:7–13 say about this?

Sin brought shame. Adam and Eve felt terrible and guilty. They were ashamed, covered themselves, and hid.

▶ **Your relationship with other people.** How did sin affect Adam and Eve's relationship with each other? How should they have treated each other instead?

Sin brought division. Adam and Eve started accusing one another, shifting the blame.

▶ **Your relationship to the space around you.** Read Genesis 3:16–19. How did sin affect Adam and Eve's responsibility to protect, cultivate, and develop their world?

> *Sin brought hardship. Because of Adam and Eve's sin, God made it difficult to live in the world he had made. They would experience painful labor (in daily work and in childbearing).*

> [16] To the woman he said, "I will surely multiply your pain in child-bearing; in pain you shall bring forth children. Your desire shall be contrary to your husband, but he shall rule over you." [17] And to Adam he said, "Because you have listened to the voice of your wife and have eaten of the tree of which I commanded you, 'You shall not eat of it,' cursed is the ground because of you; in pain you shall eat of it all the days of your life; [18] thorns and thistles it shall bring forth for you; and you shall eat the plants of the field. [19] By the sweat of your face you shall eat bread, till you return to the ground, for out of it you were taken; for you are dust, and to dust you shall return." Genesis 3:16–19

▶ **Your relationship with God.** Read Genesis 3:22–24. How did sin affect Adam and Eve's walk with the Lord?

> *Sin brought separation from God. Adam and Eve were sent away from God's presence in the garden.*

> [22] Then the LORD God said, "Behold, the man has become like one of us in knowing good and evil. Now, lest he reach out his hand and take also of the tree of life and eat, and live forever—" [23] therefore the LORD God sent him out from the garden of Eden to work the ground from which he was taken. [24] He drove out the man, and at the east of the garden of Eden he placed the cherubim and a flaming sword that turned every way to guard the way to the tree of life. Genesis 3:22–24

▶ What do you think? If it is true that sin affects everything, then what's wrong with the common piece of advice to "follow your heart"?

> *My heart, like everything else, is tainted by sin. Therefore I cannot just "go with my heart" because my heart may actually lead me astray.*

● ● ● ● **IN CLOSING** ● ● ● ● ● ● ● ● ● ● ● ●

DON'T MOVE THE GOALPOSTS

On New Year's Day 1965, the Michigan Wolverine football team defeated the Oregon State Beavers, 34 to 7. As the whistle blew, ending the Rose Bowl game, hundreds of cheering Michigan fans stormed the field. In a victory celebration they began pulling down the opponent's goalposts.

This is no small task! In American football, goalposts are thirty feet tall, with the bottom crosspiece ten feet off the ground. They also usually weigh about five hundred pounds and can withstand 115-mile-per-hour winds. But if you get a dozen people to sit or pull on them, down they come. And often people get hurt.

A bent goalpost is a great picture of how the good of Creation and the bad of the Fall fit together. Everything in the created universe has a good and intended structure (just as goalposts are meant to stand straight up). But since the Fall, people exert force to bend God's structures in their own directions, away from God's original design.[6]

Sin isn't some negative force that exists apart from creation. Instead, sin takes God's good creation and bends it. For example, lying (a bad thing) is still communication (a good thing). A criminal (a bad thing) is still a human made in God's image (a good thing). And a glutton (a bad thing) binges on food (a good thing).

As Christians, we should

1. try to understand what is good in everything.

2. reject the ways people have bent anything away from what God intended.

3. work to re-bend what has been bent by sin, bringing it closer to what God intended.

Radically Different

1. What stood out to you from the Word this week? (How has the Lord been using his Word to work in your life this week?)

2. If you tell a little child *not* to do something, what will he or she often do? Why do you think that happens?

3. In this week's reading, what was Satan's strategy when he tempted Eve? What did he try to make her think about God?

4. Why would this be effective? (Teaching Note: Instead of enjoying how much God had made, Adam and Eve were tempted to think of how much God had *forbidden*.)

5. How is Eve's temptation similar to the way we are tempted? (Make a list of various thoughts, feelings, and desires she faced in her temptation, and then make a list of how we are tempted. Often we are tempted when we decide that something God has made is more important/valuable/enjoyable than the God who made it.)

6. This week we learned about idolatry. Who can explain this to us? What is idolatry?

7. Do we commit idolatry today? If so, how? Where?

8. What areas of life do you enjoy? How would you know if any of these become too important?

> **Note:** God had given a rule to Adam and Eve: Do not eat the fruit from one tree. He had also *commanded* them to enjoy all the other fruit trees. God wanted Adam and Eve to enjoy him through eating the fruit that he allowed, and God also gave the "you can't eat from one tree" rule so that in one area of life, Adam and Eve could show that they loved God *more* than they enjoyed the good things he had made.

Next Steps

Have your students look at the closing three numbered statements in the devotional (following the words "As Christians, we should . . ."). Discuss how this week your students can live out these points related to the following topics: (1) an argument with their parents, and/or (2) your students' concern for their reputation. As time allows, you could also apply these points to other areas.

CONTENT OVERVIEW
This week looks at how Jesus's redemption reverses the effects of the Fall. Jesus came to make "all things new" (Revelation 21:5). This "new" work of Christ began with his life, death, and resurrection and will be completed after he returns. That gives us hope for life in the world to come, and it also helps us live holy and grace-filled lives today.

Note: One day, God will make an entire new creation where everything will be perfect—no sickness, no death, no temptation, no sin. Everything will be just as God had always planned. In the Bible, the Old Testament promises that God would send someone to set everything right. In the New Testament, God kept that promise by sending Jesus.

Jesus's death paid the penalty for sin, creating a way out of this old creation. His resurrection brought the new creation into our fallen world. Jesus's risen body is glorified—the first part of a new creation to come (1 Corinthians 15:20, 22). God's plan to make all things *new* has started to come true.

Aims
- To introduce the truth that Jesus didn't come only to forgive sin but also to set right everything that sin had corrupted ("making all things new")
- To help students see how they are part of the new creation that Jesus is making
- To encourage students to live in harmony with their new-creation citizenship (i.e., to be "salt and light," etc.)

Memorize
Colossians 3:7–8

GETTING STARTED
Option 1. Story Starter
Tell about an area of your life that (1) God has been changing by his grace, or (2) you have been working by his grace to redeem and restore.

Option 2. Icebreaker Idea
Show the students a picture from the internet of a messy room. Ask, "What's one thing you know you need to do to your room?" Or, "What's one thing you've lost in your room and still haven't found?" When you clean your room, isn't it satisfying to finish and see how the "new" version of the room looks so much better than before?

WEEK FOUR
NEW

COMING SOON

NEW CREATION

Let's review. When sin entered the world, it broke the good relationships that had once existed between humans and God, between humans and nature, and among humans themselves. Like adding poison to a pot of soup, everything good was tainted with bad.

But God had a plan to set everything *right*.
> Not to throw everything out . . . and make *all new things*,
> but to fix what was broken . . .   to make *all things new*.[7]

And this is our topic for the week. To make everything new, God would send his own Son, Jesus, to heal broken relationships (Colossians 1:20). Through Christ, God would reconcile everything to himself. Things that are part good and part bad would be made new and better (Revelation 21:5).

Do you like movies? Reading about Jesus's life in the Gospels (Matthew, Mark, Luke, and John) is like watching trailers previewing the great "new-creation movie" to come. Jesus brings healing, happiness, and life. And he removes sickness, suffering, and death. As we think about the newness that Jesus brings, here's a prayer for the week.

PRAYER

"Father, thank you for sending Jesus to fix this messy world and my messy life. I see good things in my life (my relationships, my decisions, my skills, my personality, my body), but I see bad things as well. Please take this good-bad combo and make it *new*. Make me more like Jesus in all areas of my life. In Jesus's name. Amen."

Day 1

What does it mean to be "new"? Read Matthew 5:13–16.

> [13] [Jesus said,] "You are the salt of the earth, but if salt has lost its taste, how shall its saltiness be restored? It is no longer good for anything except to be thrown out and trampled under people's feet. [14] You are the light of the world. A city set on a hill cannot be hidden. [15] Nor do people light a lamp and put it under a basket, but on a stand, and it gives light to all in the house. [16] In the same way, let your light shine before others, so that they may see your good works and give glory to your Father who is in heaven." Matthew 5:13–16

▶ What does Jesus mean when he says that Christians are to be "salt" and "light" in this world?

Christians are supposed to slow down the process of decay (like salt does to meat) and bring the light of the gospel into darkness. They are supposed to be cultivators of what is good, influencing the world in positive, Christ-honoring ways.

DID YOU KNOW? ● ● ●

In the ancient world, with no electricity or refrigerators, people packed meat in salt to prevent decay. And when the sun went down, without electric lights, it was really dark.

iStock.com/Olga_Mallari

◗ What does Jesus say in Matthew 5:15 is the wrong thing to do with light?

> *To hide the light*

◗ Can you think of one area of decay or darkness in which you can be salt and light today? Pray about it and ask the Lord to bring one area to mind. Write down your thoughts.

◗ As a Christian, how might you be tempted to respond (unbiblically) to the bad of darkness and decay that exists in God's good world?

> *To either embrace it or to avoid it completely*

DaY 2

God is making all things *new*. That's our topic. Read 2 Corinthians 5:17 slowly, several times.

> Therefore, if anyone is in Christ, he is a new creation. The old has passed away; behold, the new has come.
> 2 Corinthians 5:17

○ Write down the words of the verse to answer this question: What does this verse say is true for everyone who is a Christian (everyone who is "in Christ")?

They are "new creation."

○ What do you think it means to be a "new creation"?

THINK ABOUT IT

As a Christian, you live in two worlds. On your birthday, years ago, you were born into this world, a world which contains a mix of "good" and "bad." If you're a Christian, you've also been "born *again*" and belong to the world to come—the "new" creation. Since you are a citizen of the new creation, God wants you to live your life in a way that fits the new creation.

Read Ephesians 4:22–24 (below). You may also want to look up and read verses 25–32.

> ²² [God wants you] to put off your old self, which belongs to your former manner of life and is corrupt through deceitful desires, ²³ and to be renewed in the spirit of your minds, ²⁴ and to put on the new self, created after the likeness of God in true righteousness and holiness.
> Ephesians 4:22–24

▶ List at least two "old creation" actions or attitudes you should "put off" and at least two "new creation" actions or attitudes you should "put on." Ask the Lord to help you with this today.

Day 3

God has made us part of his new creation. So he also wants us to live in a way that fits our newness. Read Titus 2:9–10.

> 9 Teach slaves [servants or employees] to be subject to their masters [employers] in everything, to try to please them, not to talk back to them, 10 and not to steal from them, but to show that they can be fully trusted, so that in every way they will make the teaching about God our Savior attractive. Titus 2:9–10 NIV

● Circle the "put off" actions that these verses say that servants or employees should not do.

● Write down the "put on" actions that these verses say that servants or employees *should* do.

● Re-read verse 10 (above). As Christians live new-creation lives, what is the *reason* in this verse for doing or not doing certain things? Put the last part of this verse in your own words.

> "be subject" (i.e., obey); "try to please them;" "show that they can be fully trusted"

> So their actions and attitudes at work will display the goodness and beauty of God, our Savior.

DID YOU KNOW? • • •

If God's new creation is like a beautiful painting, your life is like the frame.

Think about a painting and a frame: a good frame enhances a work of art. It doesn't detract from it or overwhelm it. In the same way, Jesus wants your life to draw attention to the amazingly wonderful new creation he will finish one day. (And you are part of that new creation too!)

▶ When people look at you, what do they see? Do they see more "old creation" or "new creation"? Ask the Lord to use you to draw attention to the beauty of his new creation.

• • • IN CLOSING

a PiLLaR OF THE FaiTH

Here is a true story: There once lived a man named Simeon (AD 390–459). He loved God, but he didn't like the world he lived in. About seventy years before he was born it became cool to be known as a Christian. Instead of the Roman Empire trying to kill Christians (throwing them to the lions, etc.), now Christianity was the official religion of the empire. So lots of people—even people who didn't really believe in Jesus—wanted to say they were Christians.

So in Simeon's day it was hard to tell who was a real Christian and who was faking it. The "good" and the "bad" were all mixed together, like a block of marble with swirls of different colors throughout.

Then Simeon had an idea. He wanted to try to separate the good from the bad. He wanted to worship God apart from the world. So he decided to make a pillar and live on a small platform at the top of it, far out of reach of the bad world below. He wanted to live for God "upstairs," high above the everyday world "downstairs." Simeon's first pillar was nine feet tall, but that wasn't far enough. So he had another one built, this time around fifty feet off the ground. Food was sent up using a rope and pulley. He lived there for thirty-seven years!

But there was a problem with this arrangement. (Actually there were lots of problems, and bathing was not the least of them!) For starters, Simeon couldn't escape the effects of the Fall because Simeon (a sinner) took *himself* with him to the top of the pillar! But there was another issue: Jesus has redeemed his people so they can live right in the middle of this good but fallen world—to be salt and light among decay and darkness. People are not meant to live away from others in the world.

Don't be like Simeon. Christianity isn't for "upstairs" living—just for Sundays or in your daily Bible time. Christianity is an "upstairs *and* downstairs" way of life that's meant to be lived out 24-7 with other Christians in front of the world.

1. What stood out to you from the Word this week? (How has the Lord been using his Word to work in your life this week?)

2. What do you think it would be like to live in a world/society/culture where there is no more sickness, no selfishness, no death, no fighting, no misunderstandings, no temptation, no sin?

3. What does the Bible mean when it talks about "new creation"?

4. Where in the Bible does God provide a small preview of what this new creation will be like?

5. How does this new creation relate to the good-bad world that you live in now? How does this new creation relate to all the followers of Jesus?

6. What's the difference between "making all new things" and "making all things new"?[8]

7. If you are part of the new creation because you belong to Jesus, what does it mean to be "salt and light"?

8. How can people tell that you are part of this good-bad world but also part of the new creation?

9. What did Simeon (the pillar guy) get wrong? Was he "adorning" the gospel—pointing to the goodness of the new creation to come and making it look attractive to others? What did he get right? How was he living a holy life?

Next Steps

Brainstorm with your students about how *they* can engage the good-bad world around them this week as a representative of Christ's new creation. Then help them make a list of actions (and decisions, conversations, etc.) that they would do this week *if they were to live like Simeon (the pillar guy)*. (Note: These choices wouldn't necessarily be good ones.)

Once you make the list you can read them aloud, as if you are playing a game of Simeon Says (Simon Says).

CONTENT OVERVIEW

The first four weeks have been an introduction, talking about God and about Creation, Fall, and Redemption. These three realities (good, bad, and new) are like lenses through which we get clear views of life (our world, other people, ourselves, etc.). This week we begin to look through these lenses at the big topic of relationships. More specifically, we will consider our relationship to God, particularly how we listen to him while reading his Word. As the Lord speaks, we receive spiritual nourishment, but this requires that he has first helped us to see and understand what is in his Word.

Aims

- To help students understand that God's Word actively changes those who engage with it
- To remind students that we cannot truly grasp the realities God has written unless he opens the eyes of our hearts
- To encourage students that Jesus is more than able to give spiritual sight, so they should always seek his help when they read his Word.

Memorize
Colossians 3:9–10

GETTING STARTED
Option 1. Story Starter
Tell about a time when God spoke to you through his Word in a memorable or powerful way.

Option 2. Icebreaker Idea
Show the class Leon Harmon's portrait of Lincoln that appeared in his article for *Scientific American* in November 1973, titled "The Recognition of Faces." He used this as a demonstration of the minimal conditions to recognize a face. http://web.archive.org/web/20060421232319im_/http://home.earthlink.net/~wlhunt/History/Harmon.jpg

Enlarge it and hold it close to the group while they try to identify it. If they have trouble, make the image smaller or back away from the group until someone identifies it. You can also show them the original from which this pixelated version was created (Lincoln image: https://commons.wikimedia.org/wiki/Abraham_Lincoln#/media/File:Abraham_Lincoln_seated,_Feb_9,_1864.jpg).

The point is that it's easy to see something without really seeing it clearly. That's true in life, but it's also true when it comes to seeing what God has written.

WEEK FIVE
LISTENING TO GOD

What comes to mind when you think about these actions?

- Swinging a mighty hammer
- Shooting beams of fiery energy
- Wielding a razor-sharp blade
- Controlling the effects of water

These are actions of a pretty amazing team of superheroes, right? Aquaman, Thor, Ironman, and Wolverine may come to mind. (Please accept my apology for including heroes from both Marvel Comics and DC Comics in the same sentence!) But each of these actions is an image the Bible uses to describe itself.

The Bible is powerful. It's like a hammer (Jeremiah 23:29), water (Ephesians 5:26), sword (Hebrews 4:12), and fire (Jeremiah 23:29). When you open your Bible and read, it may seem like you're in control, like you're the one doing something. After all, you're the one doing the reading.

But when you read God's Word, did you know that something is being done *to you*? God is at work. He is using his Word to change you and help you.

PRAYER

"Lord, thank you for giving us your Word to speak to us. How awful life would be—how in the dark we would be—if you had been silent. Help me learn about your Word this week and to be a better listener to you. In Jesus's name I pray these things. Amen."

Day 1 (GOOD)

No surprise, but there are a lot of *good* things to say about the Bible. We've already seen that it's like a hammer, sword, fire, and water. But that's just the beginning.

Read Deuteronomy 8:3.

> And he humbled you and let you hunger and fed you with manna, which you did not know, nor did your fathers know, that he might make you know that man does not live by bread alone, but man lives by every word that comes from the mouth of the LORD.
> Deuteronomy 8:3

○ If you were explaining this verse to a first grader, what would you say?

○ Why do you think God says his Word, the Bible, is like bread (food)? Circle all that apply. Which of the following does God's Word, our spiritual food, do for you?

　✱ Makes you stronger

　✱ Improves math scores

　✱ Provides endurance

　✱ Gives health

　✱ Reduces body fat

○ God made human beings to survive not just on physical food (bread, meat, mac and cheese, etc.) but on something else. What?

> *God made people to be truly nourished by his Word. His Word gives his people life.*

God made his Word to help you. If you've not been regularly in his Word, ask the Lord to help you "eat" more often, more regularly. A healthy feast awaits you each day.

Day 2 (BAD)

Read Genesis 3:8–9.

> 8 And they heard the sound of the Lord God walking in the garden in the cool of the day, and the man and his wife hid themselves from the presence of the Lord God among the trees of the garden. 9 But the Lord God called to the man and said to him, "Where are you?" Genesis 3:8–9

▶ We've already discussed how Adam and Eve made a choice to disobey God. But *after* Adam and Eve sinned, what did they do when they heard the Lord?

> *They both hid from the Lord.*

Have you ever turned on the light and seen a bug scurry out of sight? Ever since sin entered the world (and our hearts), we've all run away from God and his Word just like the bug. Everyone is born in darkness (Romans 1:21; Ephesians 4:18) and tends to avoid the light. In fact, the Bible says that it's like all of us are born with a serious spiritual disability. We don't see clearly.

▶ Write out Psalm 119:18 (below) in your own words. Make this your own prayer.

> Open my eyes, that I may behold wondrous things out of your law. Psalm 119:18

Throughout this week, pray this short verse as a prayer to God from your heart.

Day 3 (NEW)

In the gospels Jesus healed many blind people. At the beginning of that day, they were in darkness, but after meeting Jesus, they could see! Did you know that Jesus also healed *spiritual* blindness? Read Luke 24:45.

> Then he opened their minds to understand the Scriptures.
> Luke 24:45

▶ With new spiritual sight what could these men now see?

> *They could now see clearly what God had written.*

Did you know that Jesus still heals like this today? Jesus takes away the blindness and darkness that you learned about yesterday. He is the one who gives spiritual sight and light. If you want to understand the Bible, you must first trust Jesus. He came to make all things *new*. This includes the way you read the Bible, the way you view its truths, and the way you think about God. Read Acts 26:17b–18a.

> [17] [The Lord said to Paul]"I am sending you [18] to open their eyes, so that they may turn from darkness to light and from the power of Satan to God, that they may receive forgiveness of sins." Acts 26:17b–18a

▶ Do you know a friend or family member who doesn't believe the Bible? Pray Acts 26:17b–18a for them. Pray that God gives you an opportunity to talk with them about what Jesus means to you.

IN CLOSING

OPEN YOUR EYES

It can be frustrating to be around people who never stop talking about themselves. *Me, me, me!*

And then there are the people who "*humble* brag" on social media.

I was so honored to be part of a seven-day trip to Disney . . .

#juststaythere

Honestly seeking advice on how to best spend the prize money that came with my award?

#ihaveanidea

Hating life, got pulled over in my brand new Corvette, just *looked* like I was speeding.

#wannarelieveyoursuffering

#gladlytakeitoffyourhands

The Bible is spectacular because even though it tells us about some amazing people, it doesn't brag. In fact, that's one reason you can know it's real and true.

Imagine a different scenario. What if *you* had been responsible to tell the story about Jesus's disciples (the men who would become the biggest leaders in the early church)? What would you have said about them? Would you have told about how quickly they learned from Jesus? How they showed amazing potential?

But the four Gospels (Matthew, Mark, Luke, and John) seem to go out of their way to show how messed up the disciples were. Especially when you read the gospel according to Mark, you can see that these disciples repeatedly just didn't get it (Mark 4:13; 7:17; 8:14–16). Jesus had to rebuke them (4:12–13), and eventually they abandoned Jesus for a while (14:50).

Imagine. If the gospel writers were just making up all this stuff about Jesus, why would they tell honest and some-times ugly stories about church leaders? The honesty of the Gospels shows that they weren't telling lies. Instead, they were spreading the truth about what happened, even when it showed that Jesus's followers could be weak and "blind." But the good news is that Jesus could heal their blindness then and he can heal *your* blindness today.

Keep praying for clearer spiritual sight, and keep reading his trustworthy Word. The Lord will open your eyes to see the truth. You can depend on it.

1. What stood out to you from the Word this week? (How has the Lord been using his Word to work in your life this week?)

2. What are some word pictures that God used to show us what his Word is like? (Answers: hammer [Jeremiah 23:29], water [Ephesians 5:26], sword [Hebrews 4:12], fire [Jeremiah 23:29], food [Deuteronomy 8:3].)

3. In what ways is God's Word like food? What are the points of comparison? What does food do for you? How is God's Word similar?

Note: God also tells us that his Word is like a mirror (which shows us what we are really like, James 1:23–25) and like gold (which is incredibly valuable, Psalm 19:9–10).

4. Do you need help when you read God's Word? Why?

5. What kind of help do you need? Why?

6. What does the Bible mean when it talks about spiritual "blindness"?

7. If you're spiritually blind, what will your time in the Word be like (or not like)?

8. How do you deal with this kind of spiritual blindness? (Answer: Only Jesus can heal this blindness and give spiritual sight.)

> **Note:** There are actually two types of spiritual blindness. (1) An unbeliever is spiritually blind and cannot see and appreciate the beauty and truth of the Lord. See 2 Corinthians 4:4. The answer for this blindness is "regeneration," when the Spirit gives new life and the person who believes the gospel is "born again." (2) The second kind of blindness is found in believers; it's actually more like near-sightedness. It's not uncommon for us to fail to truly see what the Lord is saying to us. See 2 Peter 1:9.

Next Steps
Give each student a note card. Instruct them to write down a prayer to the Lord, asking him to open their eyes so they can truly see and appreciate and love and trust him in his Word this week. Before they begin, explain that they need to use parts of the following verses as building blocks for constructing their prayers: Psalm 119:18; 146:8; 2 Corinthians 4:6; Ephesians 1:18.

Week Six: Talking to God

CONTENT OVERVIEW

This week introduces the topic of prayer. One way we relate to God is by talking to him. We understand prayer better when we see it through the lenses of Creation, Fall, and Redemption. Before sin entered the world, God walked and talked with Adam and Eve in the garden of Eden. He created them to talk with him. But the Fall sent mankind away from God and broke that fellowship with him. Ever since then, when people cling to sin, they are pushing away from God. But Jesus came to remove sin and restore the relationship between God and his people. We pray in "Jesus's name," that is, through what he has accomplished by his life, death, and resurrection. Communication with God was enjoyed at Creation, disrupted by the Fall, and restored through Christ's redemption.

Aims
- To assure students that God wants to hear our prayers; he created us to communicate with him
- To emphasize that treasuring sin in the heart (not merely sinning in word or deed) disrupts the enjoyment of communication with God
- To help students understand what it means to pray "in Jesus's name"

Memorize
Colossians 3:11–12

GETTING STARTED
Option 1. Story Starter
Tell about when God answered one of your prayers.

Option 2. Icebreaker Idea
We all know that prayer is talking with God. And sometimes even the youngest children understand that simplest truth about prayer.

Show the group several children's prayers (http://www.beliefnet.com/faiths/facebook-galleries/dear-god-hilarious-prayers-from-kids.aspx).

We may chuckle at these kinds of prayers—and they are funny—but what do you appreciate about these prayers? What is good and commendable about them?

WEEK SIX
TALKING TO GOD

I like detective stories, especially the ones about Sherlock Holmes. Holmes, a genius who sees important details that other people miss, uses his powers of observation to solve mysteries or capture criminals. Some stories tell how Sherlock finds a way to enter a locked or hidden room (such as in "The Red-Headed League"). And often the stories end with the detective luring someone out of hiding in order to talk with this person who had been so hard to track down (such as in the story "A Study in Scarlet").

Sometimes it's easy to think that prayer is like solving a puzzling mystery. With this mind-set, you have to work really hard to unlock a secret entrance to God. Or you have to go through careful steps in order to capture his attention and talk to him. But prayer doesn't require a hidden access code or password. And you don't have to be a spiritual genius to engage the Lord in conversation. Basically, prayer is talking with the God who wants to hear you.

PRAYER

"Thank you that in your Word, you not only talk to me, but you also help me know how to talk to you. Lord, will you please teach me to pray? Help me grow in this area of life. In Jesus's name. Amen."

Day 1 (GOOD)

Before sin entered the world, what did God think about prayer? Read Genesis 3:8.

> And they heard the sound of the LORD God walking in the garden in the cool of the day, and the man and his wife hid themselves from the presence of the LORD God among the trees of the garden. Genesis 3:8

▶ What was the Lord doing?

God himself was walking in the garden.

Apparently, God had done this before. Adam and Eve recognized who was walking in the garden. They had talked with God previously. This shouldn't be a surprise when you see what Jesus said in Matthew 7:11.

> If you then, who are evil, know how to give good gifts to your children, how much more will your Father who is in heaven give good things to those who ask him! Matthew 7:11

▶ According to this verse, how would you describe the Father's heart toward the prayers of his children?

He loves to give good gifts to his children who ask him to supply what they need.

▶ Take a moment to just tell your Father what is on your heart and mind—what's bothering you, worrying you, distracting you, or making you happy.

Day 2 (BAD)

NO SERVICE

Doesn't bad cell phone or Wi-Fi coverage drive you crazy? Did you know that sin does the same kind of thing to prayer? Read Psalm 66:18.

{ If I had cherished iniquity in my heart, the Lord would not have listened. Psalm 66:18

▶ Rephrase this verse using your own words.

▶ According to this verse, what is most true? (Circle one.) If I _____ sin, the Lord will not hear me.

commit   stumble into   (love)   struggle with

Did you know that one kind of prayer always gets through? Read Proverbs 28:13.

{ Whoever conceals his transgressions will not prosper, but he who confesses and forsakes them will obtain mercy. Proverbs 28:13

▶ What clears away this sin-barrier to prayer? What kind of prayer does God always love to hear?

> The Lord forgives and removes sin; the Lord loves to hear prayers of repentance.

▶ Are there sins that you don't want to stop doing? Do you find yourself, when you think about it, actually wanting to keep doing what *you* want to do, instead of what God wants? If so, will you confess those sins to the Lord? (See page 67 for some ideas of how this kind of confession might sound. Use the Bible's words to form your own prayer to the Lord.)

Day 3 (NEW)

Jesus opened the pathway to God. Read John 14:13.

> [Jesus said,] "Whatever you ask in my name, this I will do, that the Father may be glorified in the Son." John 14:13

▶ This verse describes a certain way to pray. According to this verse, how should you pray? Fill in the blank.

Christians pray ___*in*___ Jesus's ___*name*___.

▶ So in your own words, what does it mean when you pray "in Jesus's name"?

> When we pray in Jesus's name, we rely on all his ability and authority.

▶ Does praying in Jesus's name mean you can ask for anything you could ever possibly want? What kinds of prayers do you think *fit* "Jesus's name"? Write down two things that you can ask God for "in Jesus's name."

DID YOU KNOW? •••

When you do something in the name of someone else, you are acting as if you were in that person's shoes. (Like when someone making a citizen's arrest says, "I arrest you in the name of the law," he or she is standing in the place of the police.) Acting "in the name of" someone else means doing something as if you were the other person—using their resources, abilities, authority, and privileges.

IN THE NAME OF THE LAW...

IN CLOSING

KEEP IT FRESH

In church you might have heard some people say a lot of the same things when they pray. For example,

- "Dear heavenly Father"
- "In Jesus's name, Amen"
- "Lead, guide, and direct us"
- "We just want to thank you . . ."
- "Thank you for this day."
- "Bless the gift and the giver"

Perhaps you can think of other phrases that may have lost their meaning because they've been used so often.

But when it comes to prayer, the Bible is packed with variety. When you pray, there are even different ways to position your *body*. People pray while

- spreading arms wide (Exodus 9:29).
- lifting hands (1 Timothy 2:8).
- kneeling down (Daniel 6:10).
- bowing down on the ground (Exodus 34:8).
- lying down (Ezra 10:1).
- standing up (Genesis 24:13).
- sitting (2 Samuel 7:18).
- looking up (John 17:1).
- looking down (Luke 18:13).

And there are different ways to arrange your *words*. On the next page is a small sample of different prayers for different circumstances. However you may feel at a particular time, the Lord has provided prayers for you. He invites you to share your heart with him (Psalm 62:8).

Prayers Confessing Sin

"Have mercy on me, O God, according to your steadfast love; according to your abundant mercy blot out my transgressions. Wash me thoroughly from my iniquity, and cleanse me from my sin!" (Psalm 51:1–2; see also Psalm 40:11–12.)

Prayers Praising God

"Worthy are you, our Lord and God, to receive glory and honor and power, for you created all things, and by your will they existed and were created." (Revelation 4:11; see also 1 Chronicles 29:10–13.)

Prayers Making Requests

"And it is my prayer that your love may abound more and more, with knowledge and all discernment, so that you may approve what is excellent, and so be pure and blameless for the day of Christ, filled with the fruit of righteousness that comes through Jesus Christ, to the glory and praise of God." (Philippians 1:9–11; see also 2 Thessalonians 2:16–17.)

1. What stood out to you from the Word this week? (How has the Lord been using his Word to work in your life this week?)

2. Here's a thought experiment. If you could see the Lord's face, how do you envision he'd look while thinking about you or talking to you? (Would he seem sad, distracted, engaged, upset, frustrated, disappointed, etc.?)

3. How would it change your prayers if you knew that God really, deeply, authentically *wanted* to talk to you and to hear your concerns? Why?

4. The study this week said that when you treasure sin, God will hear only one kind of prayer from you. Does that sound right to you? How would you say it differently? What do you think the Bible teaches about this (read Psalm 66:18, see also Proverbs 15:8)?

5. As you've thought about it this week, what does it mean to pray "in Jesus's name"? What do you think it does *not* mean? (How can praying "in Jesus's name" be abused or misused by people?)

> **Note:** Praying "in Jesus's name" doesn't mean that you get *anything* you want. Only the kinds of prayers that fit Jesus are answered positively. You're praying "in his name," after all. (See James 4:3–4.) If you prayed "in Jesus's name" just to get what you wanted, that would be like arresting someone "in the name of the law," not for breaking the law, but for irritating you. In the same way, when you pray "in Jesus's name," you should pray for the things that *Jesus* wants. The Father will always hear that kind of prayer.

6. Read Matthew 6:9–13 ("the Lord's Prayer")—what kind of things or categories does Jesus want us to pray for?

7. If Jesus is eternal (no beginning, no ending) and infinite (without any limitations), how wide of a pathway do you think he has opened to the Father for us? How does this thought change the way you think about your prayers going to the Lord?

Next Steps

Make a Prayer Plan. Have each person take a few minutes to plan a time for prayer each day in the week ahead. Plans might include such things as what time of day to pray, how many minutes to dedicate for prayer, and what to pray for. They could also make a prayer card on which to list a handful of requests they would like to pray for. Encourage students to select one of the prayers from the Bible that are listed under "Keep It Fresh," at the end of this week's student devotional.

Ask some volunteers (students or leaders) to share their plan with the group. Then ask the Lord to bless and help their times in prayer this week.

CONTENT OVERVIEW

God calls his people to respond to him in ways that he defines and enables—what the Bible identifies as "worship." Worship is the *response* of who I am to a *revelation* of who God is. In the very good beginning, God created us to worship him supremely—loving, trusting, and obeying him with all of our lives. The heart of sin is when we worshipfully respond to things God has made, rather than to him. The Bible calls this misdirected worship "idolatry," which is elevating any aspect of creation to the role rightly reserved for the Creator. But Jesus has poured out his mercy on us, enabling and motivating us to worship God supremely.

Aims

- To help students realize that loving, praising, and treasuring God above all else is not a deprived life, but the fullest life
- To enable students to understand that idolatry lies at the center of all sin
- To summon students to live a complete life of worship, in response to the mercy God has shown them in Christ

Memorize

Colossians 3:13–14

GETTING STARTED

Option 1. Story Starter

Tell how the Lord taught you about the joy of worshiping him.

Option 2. Icebreaker Idea

Sometimes it's hard to know how to participate in worship services. Some people raise their hands; some don't; and some . . . well, we're not sure what's happening.

When you see people engaged in worship—whether quietly or energetically—what do you think? How do you process the actions that you see often accompany worship?

WEEK SEVEN
WORSHIPING GOD

"Everyone worships, even people who don't believe in God."

Do you agree with this statement? Is it really true? Take a moment to think it over.

The real question isn't whether everyone worships. The issue is *what* do people worship?

In other words, all people have something they love and value the most. Every person relies on something to make life work—to provide happiness or peace or whatever is desired. Everyone has a "god" who provides what he or she "needs."

For example, some people treasure *relationships*; they hope that friends will make them happy. Other people value what *achievement* can give: success, money, fame. Whatever you're hoping will give you what you most deeply want, that's what you worship, even if you don't literally kneel before it or sing songs to it.

So it's true that we all worship something.

PRAYER

"Lord, you are the true God, the only God. You made everything good, but not *best*. You are the best. Please help me believe this and live like this. Give me grace to see how amazing you are and to treasure you above everything you have created. In Jesus's name. Amen."

Day 1 (GOOD)

When your mom and dad say that something "is good for you," what do they usually mean? Aren't they saying that something will make you better, stronger, safer, or more alive? It's something that'll cause you to flourish and thrive.

Did you know that God talks like this too? Read Psalm 92:1.

> It is good to give thanks to the LORD, to sing praises to your name, O Most High. Psalm 92:1

▶ Think about this verse and write it down in your own words.

Read Psalm 147:1.

> Praise the LORD! For it is good to sing praises to our God; for it is pleasant, and a song of praise is fitting. Psalm 147:1

▶ Put these two verses together. What do Psalm 92:1 and Psalm 147:1 say about worship? How do they describe it?

> Worshiping God is appropriate, fitting, and truly good.

When you worship God, it's *good for you*! You were created to find "the good life"—the one that's full of treasuring and delighting in God with all your heart (Psalm 37:4; Mark 12:30).

Day 2 (BAD)

In the garden of Eden, Eve and Adam should have loved and treasured God more than anything else. However . . . read Genesis 3:6.

> So when the woman saw that the tree was good for food, and that it was a delight to the eyes, and that the tree was to be desired to make one wise, she took of its fruit and ate, and she also gave some to her husband who was with her, and he ate. Genesis 3:6

▶ List all the benefits that disobeying God seemed to offer Eve.

> *Disobedience seemed to offer nourishment ("good for food"), beauty ("a delight to the eyes"), and wisdom.*

▶ Were these benefits wrong in themselves? What made them sinful for Eve to pursue? (Hint: read Genesis 2:16–17.)

> *These benefits are not sinful in themselves; God created food, beauty, and wisdom. Eve was wrong in seeking these good things through creation, apart from God. She was wrong in seeking them by disobeying God, as opposed to finding them in obedience to God.*

▶ At the moment of her temptation, what was Eve treasuring most?

> *The things God created more than the Creator.*

▶ Think about something you did recently that was wrong. Why did you do it? What did you really want in your heart? Often the thing we want (treasure, worship) is one—or more—of the following:

- ❑ control
- ❑ comfort
- ❑ acceptance
- ❑ stuff
- ❑ power
- ❑ pleasure
- ❑ fame

▶ Which of these do you find yourself wanting most regularly? Pray about understanding how these things can lead you toward sin. How can you treasure the Lord more than these things?

Day 3 (NEW)

In the Old Testament, their "worship services" happened as people brought their sacrifices to the tabernacle or temple. Today you probably go to church on Sunday. But the New Testament says something amazing about worship. Read Romans 12:1.

> I appeal to you therefore, brothers, by the mercies of God, to present your bodies as a living sacrifice, holy and acceptable to God, which is your spiritual worship. Romans 12:1

▶ According to this verse, what is the "sacrifice" that God wants from you in worship today?

He's not asking for part of you or for some gift from you. Instead, God wants you to give yourself (your body), all of you.

THINK ABOUT IT

Do you realize what the Bible is saying? God doesn't need your singing or your Bible time. In fact, he doesn't need worship from you. He wants *you*—all of you! That's how you worship God—by giving your whole life, every day of the week.

▶ Re-read Romans 12:1 (above). Take a moment to write out a prayer thanking the Lord for his mercy (his love, forgiveness, and help). Because he has given everything for you, express how you want to give everything for him.

IN CLOSING

Say "aHH"

Ahhhhh! If you have ever drunk a cold soft drink on a hot day, you know this sound.

But did you know that the soda company Coca-Cola owns the internet domain name featuring the words "ahh," "ahhh," and "ahhhhh"? In fact, it actually owns all the domain names for "ahh," from two *h*'s up to 61 *h*'s.

Almost every commercial or ad that shows people drinking soda also includes those people breathing out a refreshing "ahhh"! They can't help it! It's the natural reaction to something so cool and delicious.

The "ahh" is a response the same way that worship is a response. As we come to realize who God is and what he's like (by reading his Word), we respond—not with "ahh," but in thankfulness, delight, reliance, and obedience. So if you want to improve your worship experiences, don't focus on your worship.

Instead focus on God in his Word. Ask God to give you clearer glimpses of himself. The more you see his breathtaking mercy, his authentic compassion, his limitless ability, and his brilliant insight, the more your heart will respond accordingly. That's worship.[9]

1. What stood out to you from the Word this week? (How has the Lord been using his Word to work in your life this week?)

2. How is worshiping God actually *good* for you?

> **Note:** Worship recognizes God as the most supremely good and beautiful being in the universe. So if we worship anything other than God, we love something that is less than best. And we're also living at odds with the whole arrangement of the universe, going against the grain. Worshiping God, on the other hand, fits life and is the greatest good. It also allows us to enjoy all that he has made in its proper place and priority.

3. What should you do if you don't feel like praising God? Should you repent of that sin and, asking the Lord to help you, just start praising him anyway? Why or why not?

4. What is idolatry? Do we worship idols today? Where? How?

5. What's at the heart of idolatry? (**Note:** At their core, sin problems are actually worship problems. What you treasure [worship], you pursue in life.)

6. Romans 12:1 calls us to worship not just Sundays—but where and how? How far does God want our worship to reach?

7. Read Mark 12:30, and in your own words describe how wide our treasuring of God should be.

8. Recall the Coca-Cola story in the study this week. Tell about a time when you had an "ahh" reaction in your worship of God.

9. What do you think your student book meant when it said, "If you want to improve your worship experiences, don't focus on your worship"?

Next Steps

Worship Practice. Pick one truth about the Lord that you can discuss as a group (e.g., provides food [Psalm 136:25]; gives physical strength [Isaiah 40:29]; is a refuge [2 Samuel 22:31]; promises to never leave his people [Hebrews 13:5]; satisfies the human heart [Psalm 16:11]). Briefly discuss some aspects of this truth and its significance. Then brainstorm about how to respond, whether at church, home, school, etc. What are responses to this reality about the Lord? Help your students think through how to respond to the Lord.

And here's a challenge for your students this week. When they next go to a church service, they should listen for at least one truth about Jesus Christ that they can respond to in some way (i.e., *worship*). This response may or may not have anything to do with singing.

Week Eight: Relating to Parents

CONTENT OVERVIEW

This week considers what the Bible says about how to relate to parents. In God's design, sinful parents (and that includes all of them) are typically sources of much good for their children. The joys of family are some of his biggest blessings to us. Still, even the best parents are limited and flawed—to think or wish otherwise would be unrealistic.

Yet Jesus has come not only to provide forgiveness for our sins but also to bring us into the family of God. Through Christ we belong to a new family, in addition to our earthly family. And while Jesus has instructed us to honor our earthly families, he also calls us to give higher priority to our spiritual family.

Aims

- To help students realize that even the worst parents are designed to do good in their children's lives
- To remind students that even the best parents are not perfect
- To call students to honor not merely their own mother and father but, more supremely, their heavenly Father

Memorize

Colossians 3:15–16

GETTING STARTED

Option 1. Story Starter

Tell about something your parents regularly said to you when you were growing up and how you think about it now.

Option 2. Icebreaker Idea

It's important that as you grow up, you learn to listen. What's your favorite piece of advice from your mom or dad? See if this video includes any from around your house (https://www.youtube.com/watch?v=KMRj9mvBdzw).

Why do you think your parents remind you about the advice you just mentioned?

WEEK EIGHT
RELATING TO PARENTS

I f you've ever played the game Apples to Apples, you'll know that each of the 749 red cards features both a different topic (like "Scooby Snacks" or "Florida" or "Misspelled Tattoos") and a humorous blurb to go along with it. The card titled "Stuff Your Parents Like" has this funny description: "Well, there goes something else that used to be cool."

It's hard being a kid, living with mom and dad. How uncool, right? Wouldn't it be great if you could just change one thing (or twenty!) about them? Usually friends aren't nearly as difficult to get along with. But the reality is that the deepest relationships are usually the most difficult—because you really get an up-close view of that person's strengths, limitations, and flaws. So if you can't *change* mom and dad, how do you handle your parents? The best place to start is to talk to God about it.

PRAYER

"Father, you are a good father, all the time. I really don't get my mom and dad sometimes, but you do. You made them. Please help me grow in my understanding of my parents, as well as in my love for them. Help me see them the way you see them. In Jesus's name. Amen."

Day 1 (GOOD)

Today we're going to look at God's original and **good** design for parents. Read Matthew 7:11.

> [Jesus said,] "If you then, who are evil, know how to give good gifts to your children, how much more will your Father who is in heaven give good things to those who ask him!" Matthew 7:11

❿ According to Jesus's teaching in this verse, what does any parent like to do for their children?

Parents love to provide for their children.

This means that despite the Fall, as a general rule sinful parents are still good parents. Remember the goalpost story from week three? Most moms and dads have not "bent" their role as parents beyond recognition.

❿ What is one area of goodness in your parents that you can thank the Lord for today? (Be sure to thank your mom or dad too.)

Day 2 (BAD)

The Bible agrees with you that parents don't have it all figured out. Sometimes they won't let you do what you want. And they can give what seem to be awfully weak reasons for saying no. (*arrghh!*) But God never promises that parents will be perfect. Instead, he's very realistic about it. God knows that your mom and dad are doing the best they can. Read Hebrews 12:9–10.

> ⁹ Besides this, we have had earthly fathers who disciplined us and we respected them. Shall we not much more be subject to the Father of spirits and live? ¹⁰ For they disciplined us for a short time as it seemed best to them, but he disciplines us for our good, that we may share his holiness. Hebrews 12:9–10

▶ What phrase in Hebrews 12:9–10 says that parents aren't perfect?

"as seemed best to them"

Now read Ephesians 6:1–3.

> ¹ Children, obey your parents in the Lord, for this is right. ² "Honor your father and mother" (this is the first commandment with a promise), ³ "that it may go well with you and that you may live long in the land." Ephesians 6:1–3

▶ List all the ways, given in this passage, that you should treat your parents, regardless of their imperfections.

"obey" your parents and "honor" your parents

Pause and ask the Lord to help you keep treating your parents as he wants you to.

WEEK EIGHT / DAY 2 **81**

Day 3 (NEW)

Today we look at how Jesus makes your relationship with your parents "**new**." Read Luke 14:26.

> [Jesus said,] "If anyone comes to me and does not hate his own father and mother and wife and children and brothers and sisters, yes, and even his own life, he cannot be my disciple." Luke 14:26

▶ What surprising thing does Jesus require from anyone who wants to be his follower ("my disciple")?

> *to "hate" your father and mother, etc.*

▶ How can Jesus command you to "hate" your parents? Read Matthew 10:37 (below) to explore what this "hating" looks like. Explain it in your own words.

> *"Hating" your parents means loving them less than you love Jesus; your love for your parents should seem like hate in comparison to your love for Jesus.*

> [Jesus said,] "Whoever loves father or mother more than me is not worthy of me, and whoever loves son or daughter more than me is not worthy of me." Matthew 10:37

God wants you to treat your parents with love and respect (Mark 7:10–13). But Jesus is teaching that you must love God *more* than you love your parents. Your love for your parents could seem like "hate" in comparison with your love for Jesus.

▶ Can you imagine ways you might make your family or parents a higher priority than God? (Hint: Think about things you enjoy about your family and parents. Where might these be bent and become too important?) Write down your thoughts.

IN CLOSING
HONOR YOUR PARENTS

Michael Oh had a choice to make. After becoming a Christian and going to college, he started to realize that the Lord was leading him to become a missionary. He also knew his parents wouldn't like it. Here's Michael's story in his own words.

I was a senior at the University of Pennsylvania, and after church I would often go to lunch with my parents. One Sunday, we went to a Chinese restaurant right near the campus, and I told my father that I wanted to be a missionary. And he said to me, "No." I said, "Dad, I appreciate everything you have done for me and for my sister, Tina." (My parents came to this country with three hundred dollars in their pockets, and lived in a tiny apartment over a Laundromat. And my father worked 120-hour weeks. And so I was trying to explain to my dad—this man whom I spent most of my life trying to please, to earn his love and affection—how my faith which had become so important to me had now moved me to the decision to want to be a missionary.)

So I said, "Dad, thank you for all that you've done for me and my sister. We are who we are, and we are where we are because of the sacrifices you and mom have made, but I refuse to live my life just trying to work hard so I can get into a good college and get a good job and make lots of money so that one day my kids will have every opportunity to get into a good college and get a good job so their kids can have every opportunity to get into college and get a good job and make lots of money, until Jesus returns. I refuse to live my life like that."

That was the start for me of how to understand "honor your father and mother." Your parents may say, "Choose: us or Jesus." And at that moment with fear and trembling and tears in your eyes, I pray that you will have the boldness to say, "I choose Jesus." For many that may bring the price of being disowned or even losing their very life. But Jesus makes it clear, if there is a choice, choose him."[10]

In 2004, Michael moved to Japan, where he founded a school for training pastors, a cafe, and a church-planting ministry. Since 2013, Michael has also been the leader of the Lausanne Movement, a worldwide missions organization.

1. What stood out to you from the Word this week? (How has the Lord been using his Word to work in your life this week?)

2. Why do you think Jesus said that parents are "evil" (Matthew 7:11)? What did he mean?

3. Think about the lenses of good, bad, and new. In spite of parents being sinful, what are ways your parents bring good into your life? What blessings does God provide for you through your parents?

4. In what ways did God intend parents to benefit their children? Now let's look up the following verses and write down some things you learn about God's original design for moms and dads: Psalm 103:13; 1 Timothy 5:8; Hebrews 12:7.

5. Why is it important as you grow up to realize that your parents aren't perfect?

6. How does this realization help you follow their advice and rules?

> **Note:** Your students know their parents' inconsistencies like no one else. The question is how do they handle this realization? Help them see how Hebrews 12:9–10 teaches that their parent's discipline is a reflection of the *Lord's* discipline and care for them. Unless your students are being hurt or abused (in which case they should talk to someone they trust, like a youth pastor or school principal), they need to seek to understand and thank the Lord even for the discipline and restrictions their parents give them.

7. Why did Jesus say that his followers need to "hate" their parents (Luke 14:26)? What does that even mean?

8. How does the story of Michael Oh, at the end of your study this week, illustrate what Jesus was saying about "hating" and honoring your parents?

9. How can you honor Jesus in your relationship with your parents?

Next Steps

Honor Project. Brainstorm with your students about ways they can show honor to their parents. List as many concrete ways as they come up with. Then have them write down their action plan for how they can take steps to honor their parents this week. (If your group is too big for brainstorming, divide into smaller, leader-facilitated discussion groups for this exercise.)

Try to find time at (or before) your next meeting for the students to share how their "honor project" went. If you will have the students report back at your next meeting, be sure to let them know in advance so that they can be prepared to participate.

CONTENT OVERVIEW

This week's topic is friends. God has given human friendship as an expression of his kind heart toward us. The goodness of human relationships is his idea. Because we're sinners, we're not always the kind of friends we should be. Yet Jesus sacrificed his life to remove our sins and draw us into friendship with *him*. As a result of his life-changing friendship to us, we are able to be that same kind of friend, loving others like Jesus has loved us.

Aims
- To encourage students to enjoy the friendships God has put into their lives
- To warn students to avoid being bad friends
- To call students to be good friends—to enjoy and exemplify the loving and helpful friendship Jesus has personally made with them

Memorize
Colossians 3:17

GETTING STARTED
Option 1. Story Starter
Tell about one of your best friends you had when you were growing up and something memorable you did together.

Option 2. Icebreaker Idea
Friendship Game. Divide the group into two or more teams. Give each group a sheet of paper and a pen. The goal of the game is to see which team can come up with the most pairs of famous friends. Here are some examples: Tom and Jerry; Abbott and Costello; Charlie Brown and Snoopy; Pooh and Piglet; Kirk and Spock; Hermione Granger and Harry Potter (or Ronald Weasley); etc.

As you think about your list, what makes for a good friendship? (Make a list of the answers given.)

WEEK NINE
RELATING TO FRIENDS

Texting can be awesome . . . and annoying. Tech-challenged family members might send "lots of love" (LOL), and some friends just can't take a hint!

> Hi!!!!!!!!
>
> Whatsup?????
>
> How was your night?
>
> ?????
>
> Whatcha doing today?
>
> Headed to a friends!

But, on the positive side, your phone can be an easy way to keep in touch with friends. Obviously friendships have been around a lot longer than texting or the latest app. This week we're going to look at what the Bible says about friendship.

PRAYER

"Father, thanks for the friends you've given to me. Help me be a good friend to those who need friends. Most of all let me learn to enjoy Jesus's friendship more. In his name. Amen."

Day 1 (GOOD)

▶ If you took special time to spend just with God—reading his Word and talking to him—where would you go? What would you do? Stop and try to imagine the most spiritual and godly scenario you can dream up.

It's hard to think of anything better than what God created for Adam in the garden of Eden. Here's what Adam enjoyed: no distractions or difficulties, only the most stunning surroundings, good food, fun stuff to do, and the closest relationship with God. It was all very good, which makes what God said next so incredibly surprising. Read Genesis 2:18a.

> Then the LORD God said, "It is not good that the man should be alone." Genesis 2:18a

Without *other people*, even the best life—and the best Christian life—would be incomplete. God designed you to enjoy friendship.

▶ How can friendship help you? Read Ecclesiastes 4:9-10 and Proverbs 27:17 and write down an answer. Add other ideas that come to mind.

> Two are better than one, because they have a good reward for their toil. For if they fall, one will lift up his fellow. But woe to him who is alone when he falls and has not another to lift him up! Ecclesiastes 4:9-10
>
> Iron sharpens iron, and one man sharpens another. Proverbs 27:17

▶ Take 45 seconds and thank the Lord for providing friends (or ask him to provide friends).

Day 2 (BAD)

God gave you friends. After all, the whole concept of friendship was his idea! Friends help each other, enjoy each other, and encourage each other. But, as you know, friends can be difficult too.

▶ Describe some characteristics of a not-so-good friend. What do you think a bad friend is like?

▶ Read Proverbs 16:28 and Psalm 38:11 (below). What are some things that make for a bad friend according to these verses?

Spreading gossip and not giving encouragement or providing helpful support.

{ A contrary person spreads conflict, and a gossip separates close friends. Proverbs 16:28 CSB

My loved ones and friends stand back from my affliction, and my relatives stand at a distance. Psalm 38:11 CSB

▶ How do you think your friends would describe you?

● Give two specific and recent examples of how you have not been a good friend.

● Take some time to talk to the Lord about how you could be a better friend. Is there anything you need to ask him or others to forgive you for?

Day 3 (NEW)

Friends are part of God's good design for life in this world. They help you and encourage you. The wrong kind of friends may influence you in bad directions. But Jesus came not just to give you good friends but to help make *you* into a good friend. How? Let's dive in.

▶ Read John 15:12–13. What do these verses show you about what Jesus's death has done to transform your relationship with him? How does he set the best example for friendship?

> *Jesus sets the ultimate example of a friend sacrificing his life for others. Friendship pursues self-sacrifice, giving up preferences, choices, comfort, time, etc.*

{ [Jesus said,] "This is my commandment, that you love one another as I have loved you. Greater love has no one than this, that someone lay down his life for his friends." John 15:12–13

Jesus didn't die to make good people, attractive people, or nice people into his friends. He came to die for sinners—men and women who were born with the desire to go their own way, instead of God's way (Romans 5:6, 10).

▶ If you belong to Jesus, if he has brought you into friendship with God, what's your plan to be the kind of friend Jesus has been to you? How will you be the kind of friend who befriends even those who are needy, who don't have much in common with you, who can't pay you back? (Jesus talks about this in Luke 14:12–14.)

IN CLOSING

aLL iN THE SaME BOaT

In his book, *The Boys in the Boat*, Daniel James Brown tells the all-but-forgotten adventure of nine young men in their unlikely quest to win the gold medal in rowing for the United States at the 1936 Berlin Olympics. Leading up to this Olympic pursuit, the story follows the life of Joe Rantz, who rose from a difficult past and dysfunctional family to find in his teammates a brotherhood of friends.

It didn't take Joe long to discover that rowing was not a solo sport. Rowing wasn't about him. He had to focus on others. Victory required eight individuals to each fill his own unique role yet in perfect harmony and coordination with the team. Together these eight young men learned to work together. They sacrificed their own comforts, their own styles, their own desires—for the good of others. They were friends, and they were teammates.

And that's what made them so unbeatable!

> ❝[When] all were merged into one smoothly working machine; they were, in fact, a poem of motion, a symphony of swinging blades. . . . If one fellow in an orchestra was playing out of tune, or playing at a different tempo, the whole piece would naturally be ruined.❞[11]

True friends serve others. With the Lord's help and example, they don't focus on themselves, and they don't focus on the weaknesses of others. They sacrifice themselves for the success of others.

1. What stood out to you from the Word this week? (How has the Lord been using his Word to work in your life this week?)

2. Is it okay or a sign of weakness that you need other people, that you need friends?

3. What do you like about your friendships?

4. In what ways do friends influence you? Their words? Their examples? Can you think of times when you realized you were being influenced by friends?

> **Note:** Friends can help you move toward the Lord, or they can push you away from him. The Bible tells real-life stories about this kind of spiritually dangerous friend. You can read some in Genesis 38:12–23 and 2 Samuel 13:1–6.

5. What are some characteristics of people you might think of as "bad friends"? Which of these actions or attitudes are easiest for you to slip into?

6. What does it mean that Jesus's death has made you his friends? (List all the ways your group can imagine of what friendship with Jesus looks like.)

> **Note:** Jesus's death, at great cost to himself, changes enemies into friends—and has forever changed the nature of friendship. Read Luke 14:12–14, and discuss the ways Jesus has transformed friendship.

7. What are characteristics of a good and godly friend?

8. Let's make a list of ways you can be a friend who influences others toward the Lord. How can you be "a light in the darkness"?

9. How can you, like Jesus, make sacrifices to serve others and be their friend?

Next Steps
Have students complete the following statement: "Because of Jesus's friendship to me, I want to be a friend who _____." Discuss together what your students wrote and what they meant by it. You could also ask about the story behind what they wrote.

CONTENT OVERVIEW

This week is about family relationships, especially those that tend toward conflict. Because of such close proximity, family relationships often present challenges that aren't as common in more casual relationships. However, the conflict that may seem unique to family relationships is actually the same as any other kind of conflict—rising from the desires of the heart (James 4:2). Yet in God's good design and despite the common challenges, family relationships have the potential to become wonderful, lifelong friendships. And, regardless of our family relationships, Jesus has placed all his followers in *his* family, which is filled with "brothers and sisters" in Christ.

Aims

- To remind students that family members are designed by God to be sources of help and encouragement
- To help students understand and handle conflict as a heart problem, not just an unavoidable family problem
- To encourage students to enjoy the wider family that they have in Christ

Memorize
Colossians 3:18–20

GETTING STARTED
Option 1. Story Starter
Tell a story about when you've experienced conflict with a family member (or close friend).

Option 2. Icebreaker Idea
Read the following "top five unique things about people in families":

- Number Five: Who else would borrow your stuff . . . without asking . . . and not bring it back!
- Number Four: Who else would feel free to keep going into your room!
- Number Three: Who else would feel comfortable saying embarrassing things in front of your friends!
- Number Two: Who else has such great taste in what shows to watch!
- And finally, Number One: Who else could possibly come close to that amount of time spent in the restroom!

What is at least one thing that you can say about your family relationships (or about very close friendships) that is unique *and positive* about them? What do you honestly appreciate?

WEEK TEN
RELATING TO FAMILY

I am the older brother to three younger sisters. Before the youngest was born, I had hoped for a brother, but alas, I got another sister. (On the other extreme, my wife grew up with two brothers and no sister.) And during my growing-up years, I have to admit there were times that we fought and argued. But mostly we just got on each other's nerves.

When we were younger, I would tease them and call them names that annoyed them. Then I would hide their toys just to watch them get frustrated. ("Brother" is, after all, only one letter away from "bother.")

Of course, when I would get in trouble, they would laugh at me—where I could see them but our parents could not. It seemed that Ephesians 4:32 was our mother's favorite verse ("Be kind to one another . . . ").

But over time something strange happened. We actually began to enjoy each other. Seem impossible with someone in *your* family? How does this kind of thing happen? That's something we'll explore this week. But first, let's pray about it.

PRAYER

"Father, you made everything according to your good design. And those plans include members of my family. Please help me see more clearly just how good you designed my family. In Jesus's name. Amen."

Day 1 (GOOD)

● You're going to like this verse. Read Proverbs 17:17 (below) and write it down word-for-word, but substitute some names of your family members in place of the word "brother."

{ **A friend loves at all times, and a brother is born for adversity.** Proverbs 17:17

After writing this verse you might say, "Yup, he or she was born for *adversity*." And it may seem like your brother, sister, or other family member was put on planet Earth just to make your life difficult. But this verse actually says the opposite of what you may have thought.

This verse teaches that when life gets difficult, your family members are there to help. God gave family to you as a gift. They help you in tough times, in "adversity."

○ Can you think of a time (any time) that someone in your family helped you when you were having a hard time? Describe in detail what you remember.

○ What can you do to be that kind of help to others today (perhaps a family member or a friend)? Pray about it and write down some ideas.

Day 2 (BAD)

Read Genesis 4:2–8 (below). This is the story of the first family, the first set of brothers. Yet its truths fit any relationship.

> ² And again, she bore his brother Abel. Now Abel was a keeper of sheep, and Cain a worker of the ground. ³ In the course of time Cain brought to the LORD an offering of the fruit of the ground, ⁴ and Abel also brought of the firstborn of his flock and of their fat portions. And the LORD had regard for Abel and his offering, ⁵ but for Cain and his offering he had no regard. So Cain was very angry, and his face fell. ⁶ The LORD said to Cain, "Why are you angry, and why has your face fallen? ⁷ If you do well, will you not be accepted? And if you do not do well, sin is crouching at the door. Its desire is contrary to you, but you must rule over it." ⁸ Cain spoke to Abel his brother. And when they were in the field, Cain rose up against his brother Abel and killed him. Genesis 4:2–8

▶ Why do you think Cain became angry with Abel? It may help to go back and re-read the story.

God rejected Cain's offering but accepted Abel's offering. Cain was jealous because he had desired something (God's approval of his offering) but did not get it.

○ Now read James 4:2 (below). Circle the word *want* in this verse.

{
You want what you don't have, so you scheme and kill to get it. You are jealous of what others have, but you can't get it, so you fight and wage war to take it away from them. Yet you don't have what you want because you don't ask God for it. James 4:2 NLT

○ In your own words, what reason does this verse give for why fights take place?

> We fight either in order to get what we want or because we didn't get what we wanted.

○ Based on today's verses, think about your relationship with family members (or even close friends). What kinds of things do you fight or argue about? What "want" or desire might be at the heart of your conflict? Take a minute to talk to the Lord about this "want."

Day 3 (NEW)

▶ Read Luke 8:19–21 (below). In these verses, who is trying to get to Jesus while he is teaching the Word of God to those crowded around him?

> *Jesus's mother and brothers*

> 19 Then his mother and his brothers came to him, but they could not reach him because of the crowd. 20 And he was told, "Your mother and your brothers are standing outside, desiring to see you." 21 But he answered them, "My mother and my brothers are those who hear the word of God and do it." Luke 8:19–21

▶ Read these verses again. What did someone say to Jesus that was intended to encourage him to wrap things up and talk to his family?

> *Your mother and brothers are waiting for you.*

▶ What surprising thing does Jesus say back?

> *My family is made up of all those who hear and obey God's Word.*

▶ Even if you have terrible family members or no family at all, if you are a Christian you are part of God's family. Thank the Lord for making you part of his own family. Then write down one way you can encourage one of your brothers or sisters in Christ, this week.

· · · · **IN CLOSING** · · · · · · · · · · · · · · · ·

BROTHERLY LOVE?
Check all that apply.

☐ **You are regularly annoyed by an individual in your family.**
☐ **You have pulled an awesome prank on a member of your family.**
☐ **You have thought about trying to sell a family member at a garage sale.**

If you've checked any of these boxes, keep reading. The reality is that it's hard to get along with people you're around all the time. You know everything about them—and every bit of it drives you crazy. That's just how family can be sometimes.

But did you know that it's pretty common for family members to actually become good friends, especially as they get older? Hopefully, you already consider your brothers or sisters or other family members as friends. But the older you get, the better friends they can become.

Did you also know that during your whole lifetime, some of the people who have known you the longest will probably be those in your family? When you're seventy (hard to imagine, I know!), you will have known your siblings or cousins, for example, for almost that entire time. And almost no one else will have known you that long.

Here are some good relationship guidelines for getting along with people in your family. (These guidelines apply to friends too.)

1. Always treat the other person with respect and thoughtfulness. (They are created in God's image, remember?)

2. If something doesn't belong to you, you usually have no reason to touch it. (Don't mess with other people's stuff without their permission.)

3. If you're trying just to have a little fun, and it's not fun for the other person, then don't do it.

4. Don't have fun or make a joke at the expense of another person.

5. Wherever possible, take the initiative to move toward people and problems in love and wisdom.

6. Privileges (like owning stuff, being older, stronger, smarter, etc.) bring greater opportunities to serve other people (including people in your family).

1. What stood out to you from the Word this week? (How has the Lord been using his Word to work in your life this week?)

2. What did you think about Proverbs 17:17? Did this verse confuse you at all?

3. If God designed family members to help each other, why do we often have so many fights and disagreements with each other?

4. What did you get from the story about Cain and Abel?

5. Is this story just about brothers? What else is going on here? What is at the heart of the problem in the Cain and Abel story?

> **Note:** While the story of Cain and Abel is not primarily about a family problem (instead it's more about the sin that can damage any relationship), the issues of anger and jealousy have been a problem in families ever since. One challenge within families (or circles of close friends) is making everything a competition— wanting to do more, have more, or be loved more than each other. When competition becomes too hot, the Bible calls this "envy" (Galatians 5:26).

6. How do you think James 4:2 fits into this discussion?

7. So when you argue, what is really going on? How would you describe what is going on under the surface?

8. What are things that siblings or friends might envy in others? (Examples include cell phones and other tech items, shoes and clothes, skills and abilities, personalities, popularity, acceptance by a friend or group, etc.)

> **Note:** When you become a Christian, you are forgiven and your sins cleaned away. But when you repent of your sin and trust Jesus as your rescuer, God also becomes your Father and you become part of his family (2 Corinthians 6:18). And since you're not the only Christian within God's family that means you have new brothers and sisters (1 Timothy 5:1–2).

9. What does it mean for us to treat other Christians as "brothers and sisters"— as family? (Read and discuss 1 Timothy 5:1–2.)

Next Steps

Read Philippians 2:3–4 to the group. Take a few minutes to gather prayer requests from your students, and then pray about their relationships with their family members (or close friends) in light of these verses. Have them write down ways they can continue praying during the week ahead.

After prayer, brainstorm together how to live out these verses by helping and serving family or friends today.

Week Eleven: Difficult Relationships

CONTENT OVERVIEW

This week tackles the topic of "difficult people." It's far too easy to find certain people annoying. This week's devotional study discusses how God views and wants us to view people—even those who are somewhat unpleasant from our self-oriented perspective. God has given every person value and a set of strengths. Each person also has a corresponding set of weaknesses and limitations. No one is an exception to these realities, except Jesus—the perfect human who laid down his life for our sins and weaknesses. He also set us an example by washing the feet of his disciples, who were displaying some rather difficult characteristics.

Aims

- To remind students that every person—even ones we find "difficult"—have God-given strengths and values to be recognized and appreciated
- To help students understand that limitations in other people are not oddities to be despised but are common in all of us
- To encourage students to rely on and model the sacrificial love of Jesus displayed when he washed his disciples' feet

Memorize

Colossians 3:21–22

GETTING STARTED

Option 1. Story Starter

Tell a story about something you do (or have done) that other people have told you is annoying.

Option 2. Icebreaker Idea

A few days before your discussion, ask one or more of your adult leaders to send you some facts about themselves that others have said they find difficult or annoying. (The leaders should include facts that can be shared with the group and written in such a way that doesn't give away their identity.) Then, at the next meeting with your students, read those facts, and ask the students to guess which leader is being described.

We all have stories we could tell about how we have been annoying, even unintentionally. And if you don't, you will eventually. We might find certain people difficult, but we all can be that difficult person from someone else's perspective. That's just the way life is.

WEEK ELEVEN
DIFFICULT RELATIONSHIPS

Every person is different . . . Some are just more different than others.

At least it seems that way. Being around some people may make you want to scream! So what grates on you the most? The sloppy, messy slob? The smacking, noisy eater? The loud laughing jokester? The social media goofball? The emotional drama king or queen?

Don't we all find different things (and people) annoying? Wouldn't it be great if everyone were more normal? More like us?

Does the Bible even talk about difficult people? Let's find out.

PRAYER

"Father, would you help me learn how to relate to people that I find difficult to be around? Would you give me love and patience with them— just as you treat me with love and patience? In Jesus's name. Amen."

Day 1 (GOOD)

▶ Read Psalm 139:14–16. According to verse 14, what words describe how God has made each person (even people whom you may think of as "difficult")?

> *Each person is made remarkably and wondrously.*

> ¹⁴ I will praise you because I have been remarkably and wondrously made. Your works are wondrous, and I know this very well. ¹⁵ My bones were not hidden from you when I was made in secret, when I was formed in the depths of the earth. ¹⁶ Your eyes saw me when I was formless; all my days were written in your book and planned before a single one of them began. Psalm 139:14–16 CSB

▶ Re-read verse 16. How much of your life, and everyone else's life (even people very different than you), has been carefully designed by God?

> *All of it; "all my days were . . . planned"*

THINK ABOUT IT

God made each human as a unique individual. There are no identical thumbprints; there are no identical people. Each person has his or her special mix of talents, personality, experiences, and family characteristics. You might find someone especially annoying who is very *different* than you, or who is actually quite *similar* to you in some way.

So, when you're around that difficult person, of course the things you find obnoxious come through loud and clear. But you're probably missing what's not so obvious to you. What are that person's *strengths*? Their *good* qualities? Remember, God has made each person in his image (Genesis 1:27), and he's also given them wonderful qualities you may not have recognized yet.

► So stop and think about a difficult person in your life. Now, without mentioning his or her name, what good qualities does this person have? What are his or her strengths?

Day 2 (BAD)

Read Mark 10:13–16.

> ¹³ And they were bringing children to him that he might touch them, and the disciples rebuked them. ¹⁴ But when Jesus saw it, he was indignant and said to them, "Let the children come to me; do not hinder them, for to such belongs the kingdom of God. ¹⁵ Truly, I say to you, whoever does not receive the kingdom of God like a child shall not enter it." ¹⁶ And he took them in his arms and blessed them, laying his hands on them. Mark 10:13–16

○ Why do you think the disciples didn't want parents to bring their children to Jesus? (Hint: Think about little kids and think about the busy schedule of Jesus's ministry.)

> *The disciples thought that Jesus was too busy and little children were unimportant and would interrupt Jesus's ministry.*

○ Here's the point: If there's light, there's shadow. Where there's strength, there's weakness. How did Jesus respond—and how should you respond—to the weakness and limitations in the story above?

> *Jesus responded by calling the little children to himself. We should always make room for even those whom people might consider weak or limited.*

Pray about how you can treat others (with their weaknesses and limitations) today.

Day 3 (NEW)

Jesus gives us (1) the example to imitate and (2) the strength to deal with difficult people. Read John 13:3–9, 12 (below). Underline the parts of the story (words/actions) that might have annoyed you if you had been there.

> ³ Jesus . . . laid aside his outer garments, and taking a towel, tied it around his waist. ⁵ Then he poured water into a basin and began to wash the disciples' feet and to wipe them with the towel that was wrapped around him. ⁶ He came to Simon Peter, who said to him, "Lord, do you wash my feet?" ⁷ Jesus answered him, "What I am doing you do not understand now, but afterward you will understand." ⁸ Peter said to him, "You shall never wash my feet." Jesus answered him, "If I do not wash you, you have no share with me." ⁹ Simon Peter said to him, "Lord, not my feet only but also my hands and my head!" . . .¹² When he had washed their feet and put on his outer garments and resumed his place, he said to them, "Do you understand what I have done to you?" John 13:3–9, 12

◗ How does Jesus respond to Peter (in word and in action)?

Jesus humbly served Peter. He also patiently explained to Peter what he was doing and why it was important.

◗ If you are a Christian, list five ways that Jesus has served and helped you.

◗ List five ways you can try to help others today (even difficult people).

IN CLOSING

JESUS RECOGNIZES THE TOUCH OF FAITH

During Jesus's ministry, there was a time that he and his disciples were trying to squeeze their way through a packed crowd of people (Mark 5:24–31). It was elbow-to-elbow crowding, pushing, and inching along. And in the middle of all that, a woman who needed healing reached out and touched Jesus's coat.

And she was instantly healed! Jesus knew what had happened, and he wanted to talk to the healed woman. So he asked, "Who touched me?" The disciples had no clue about any of this. They said something like, "Everyone's pushing and shoving, and you ask, 'Who touched me?'"

You can almost see Jesus smiling at his disciples' comment as he turned to speak with the healed woman. Even in a situation that many might find annoying, Jesus found an opportunity to serve.

1. What stood out to you from the Word this week? (How has the Lord been using his Word to work in your life this week?)

2. Ask your students to take a minute to prepare answers to these questions that they can share with the group: What is one of your strengths and abilities? What is one of your weaknesses and limitations?

> **Note:** the right group may be able to contribute as well, e.g., "What do you think some of Tonya's strengths are?" etc.

3. How would you like other people to respond to your weaknesses and limitations?

4. What different kinds of people are listed in Genesis 4:20–22? How were they unique?

5. Why do you think we find certain people difficult or annoying?

6. In the stories from the Gospels of Mark and John, what were Jesus's followers doing that seems unpleasant or difficult to you?

7. How did Jesus respond to his followers? How do you think Jesus thinks about people you may find "difficult"?

8. Read 1 Thessalonians 5:14. Which parts of this verse describe what Jesus did in the story you read in John 13?

9. How should you treat people you find difficult? How can you rely on the Lord's help and grace to strengthen you to serve and love even "difficult" people?

Next Steps

Inquire if anyone in the group ever had another person take time to wash one or both of their feet? (Perhaps you could even literally wash feet as a hands-on example for the group.)

Have everyone write down ten ways they can serve someone else this week. Ask your students to share some of what they have written, and if possible, record the list on a board for the group to see. Hopefully, some concrete next steps will emerge. End the time in prayer, asking the Lord to forgive you for proud attitudes and to help you serve others.

Teacher Guide
Week Twelve: Broken Relationships

CONTENT OVERVIEW

This week we will examine the difficulty of broken relationships. Sometimes our relationships are strained because we find others so different from us. At other times, sin clouds our view of others, and resentment or envy damages our relationships even further. Yet Jesus came to restore not only our relationship to God but also our relationships with others.

Aims

- To remind students that God created individuals to be different and unique
- To show students how sin can warp our view of others
- To help students think about how the gospel has united all followers of Christ

Memorize

Colossians 3:23–24

GETTING STARTED
Option 1. Story Starter

Tell about how you have felt the pain of a broken relationship (perhaps in your circle of family or friends) and tried to navigate the difficulty of that situation.

Option 2. Icebreaker Idea

Give everyone who wants to participate a handful of rubber bands. Then say:

"Welcome to the Rubber-Band-O-Rama. You have one minute to shoot. Take aim. Starting in three, two, one . . . go!"

Let everyone shoot for sixty seconds. Collect and redistribute the rubber bands. Give the exact same speech as before, but this time just before you say "Go!" post a large bull's-eye target within everyone's range. (Don't let your group see the target before this reveal.)

After sixty seconds, stop the group and discuss any differences they noticed between the two rounds. Also, discuss why there were differences.

> **Note:** In the first round, participants will likely shoot at each other. In the second round some may continue to shoot at each other, but many will focus instead on the target. Discuss how relationships become broken (by taking shots at each other), especially when we're not aiming at the Lord's priorities for our lives.

Isn't it easy to find yourself in one situation taking aim at others, and in a very similar situation not to be shooting at others? Relationships are easily broken or damaged, but sometimes it doesn't take much to make the difference between a good relationship and a hostile one.

WEEK TWELVE
BROKEN RELATIONSHIPS

When I was in college, my car was a ten-year-old Toyota Corolla. It had been white when it was new. Yet not even the passing of years could change that it was just a compact station wagon. Ugly car . . . but I loved it!

It didn't matter that it had been my *dad's* car, because now it was *my* car. I could drive where and when I wanted. I could go out to eat with my friends and go home on the weekends. But there were also problems.

After awhile, the car didn't start when I turned the key. I tried to get it fixed, but that didn't last. So I could never tell when it would start and when it wouldn't. My friends and I would pray and try to start it. When it didn't start, we'd give it a push in order to jump-start it. Eventually, we began calling it the "prayer mobile." It was great to have a car, but a lot of trouble too.

But car troubles don't compare to *people troubles*. There's a good chance that most of the drama in your life is related to people, not stuff. Parents, friends, teachers, relatives—these characters in life bring the highest joys and deepest pain.

Why are so many problems today related to people? It's not new. Conflicts and issues between people have been around since the beginning of human history. What do you do about it? That's what we're going to look at this week.

PRAYER

"Lord, help me think more clearly about the people in my life, especially in those relationships that seem broken. Help me act more kindly too. For Jesus's sake. Amen."

Day 1 (GOOD)

▶ Read Genesis 2:20 (below). In this verse, underline the words that describe Adam's wife.

{ He [Adam] gave names to all the livestock, all the birds of the sky, and all the wild animals. But still there was no helper just right for him. Genesis 2:20 NLT

God prepared Adam for Eve by having him name all the animals. After identifying each kind, Adam knew that none of these creatures was "just right" for him. However, Eve was another story. As another human, Eve was like Adam. Yet she was different from him—he was man and she was woman. Alike, yet not alike (Genesis 2:21-23).

Even before sin came into the world, God designed people to get along with others who were like, but not exactly like, them. Differences in people are his idea.

▶ Are your friends all the same as you are? Do you have trouble having relationships with people who are different from you? Write out a prayer asking God to help you see others as God sees them. Ask God to help you appreciate differences in the people he created.

Day 2 (BAD)

Read Genesis 3:12–13. In this passage, look for the effect that sin had on Adam and Eve's relationship.

> The man said, "The woman whom you gave to be with me, she gave me fruit of the tree, and I ate." Then the LORD God said to the woman, "What is this that you have done?" The woman said, "The serpent deceived me, and I ate."
> Genesis 3:12–13

▶ Adam and Eve had both sinned and, feeling guilty, hid from God. What did Adam say when the Lord confronted him with his sin? Did he protect and support Eve?

> Adam says that Eve tempted him to sin. He does not protect his wife; he puts the blame on her.

▶ How would you describe Adam's words? (circle one)

loving

lying

(blaming)

helping

comforting

▶ Sin was pushing Adam and Eve apart. Now think about yourself and people you know. How does sin push you away from people who are different from you?

▶ How do you think about kids in different economic circumstances from you? If they have more than you do, does envy cloud your thinking about who they really are and what they might be struggling with? Or, if they have less than you do, does pride tempt you to feel better than them?

Day 3 (NEW)

▶ Read Ephesians 2:14, 16 (below). What reason do these verses give for Jesus's death on the cross?

> *Jesus's death brings unity and reconciliation between even former enemies. He removes hostility and makes peace.*

{ For he [Jesus] is our peace, who made both groups one and tore down the dividing wall of hostility . . . He did this so that he might reconcile both to God in one body through the cross by which he put the hostility to death. Ephesians 2:14, 16 CSB

☇ DID YOU KNOW?

Jesus has united all people who follow him—even people from different countries, cultures, and groups—into one group. This means that as a Christian, you have more in common with other Christians who are super different from you than you have with your closest friend who is not a Christian.

▶ Think of someone you know who is a Christian but who is also quite different from you. List some things you have in common because you are both Christians.

▶ If your relationship with this person is broken, what next steps should you take to try to restore that relationship? (This can be difficult to handle. You may want to discuss it with a parent, teacher, or pastor.)

IN CLOSING

KEEPING YOUR BALANCE

In 2007, Sam Wakeling did something no one had ever done before. He pedaled 105.57 miles across the country of Wales without his feet ever touching the ground. That's a long distance, but people ride that far all the time. What made Sam's ride unique—a world's record actually—was that he covered those miles riding a unicycle! Not a bicycle with two wheels—a unicycle, with only *one wheel*.

Now that's an accomplishment. Keeping your balance for that long is no simple feat. Unicycle riders are constantly trying to keep from falling forward and backward, not just balancing from side to side as on a regular bike.

The same balance is needed in challenging relationships. When someone else is being difficult, you can be tempted to *be angry*. At other times you want to *run away*. The first option goes on the offensive, and the second goes into hiding.

In most cases, God wants us to stay engaged and stay calm—to be lovingly truthful and helpful. It takes balance to keep from sliding off into either attack mode or escape mode. Christian author Ken Sande says that in conflict there are three kinds of people: peace-breakers, peace-fakers, and peace-makers.[12]

KEEPING BALANCE IN CHALLENGING RELATIONSHIPS

> Pick a spot on the slope. Where would you locate your own typical response to difficult people?

1. What stood out to you from the Word this week? (How has the Lord been using his Word to work in your life this week?)

2. What are some kinds of relationships that break? (e.g., boyfriend/girlfriend; husband/wife; parent/children; friends; employee/employer; student/teacher.)

3. What kinds of things make relationships start to unravel?

4. Is it easier to get along with people who are like you or different from you? Why? How does sin distort our view of other people?

> **Note:** Because of sin, God-given good differences between peoples' personalities can become awful, not special. If someone seems really strange to you, isn't it easy to be suspicious of them? But these people we might view as different are often the ones God wants us to help. In fact, sometimes sin distorts our view of other people in a different way. Some of your students may see others as completely "normal," while these others struggle deeply with pain, guilt, anxiety, or depression. In August 2017, *Time Magazine* reported the following disturbing statistics: "From 2007 to 2015 alone, suicide rates doubled among teen girls and [increased] by more than **30 percent** among teen boys."[13]

5. What role does Jesus have in healing broken relationships? How is Jesus (and his death by which sinners are forgiven) necessary for restoring relationships?

6. How do you tend to handle conflict with another person? Are you a peace-faker, peace-breaker, or peace-maker?

7. When you sin against someone, and the relationship is broken, what should you do to help restore that relationship?

Next Steps

Help students think about how to apologize. Merely saying "I'm sorry," or "I apologize," doesn't go far enough—you haven't asked to be forgiven. Here are some biblical elements to include when making things right with someone you have sinned against. Discuss with students or have them role play to practice.

- **Own your sin.** Admit that you were wrong. (Say: "I was wrong when I _____.")
- **Feel the weight.** Try to show that you understand how your sin affected the other person. (Say: "When that happened, I'm sure you felt _____.")
- **Ask for forgiveness.** "Will you forgive me?" (This asks the other person to not hold your sin against you and aims to restore the relationship.)

CONTENT OVERVIEW
God calls each of us to be part of a larger group—the local church. Yet even the church is not immune from squabbles and sins (see 1 Corinthians!). In spite of these problems, Jesus still claims the church as his own. In the gospel, believers are more defined by what Christ has done for us than by our failures and weaknesses. As a result we should understand the church as a greenhouse for growing people, not a display case for people who are fully mature.

Aims
- To remind students that Christianity is meant to be lived in connection with other people, not as a solo pursuit
- To clarify that even Christians, who should know better, fail to live in harmony with the gospel
- To encourage students that Christ welcomes imperfect people into his family (and is working to change them to be more like himself)

Memorize
Colossians 3:25—4:1

GETTING STARTED
Option 1. Story Starter
Tell how you have been encouraged by someone at church, perhaps someone you didn't expect to receive encouragement from.

Option 2. Icebreaker Idea
Blindfold a few volunteers who are willing to sample some fruit. (Be sure to check for allergies first.) After each tasting, ask each volunteer to describe what they tasted. Have several varieties of fruit available, including a ripe banana and an unripe banana. Give tastes of both kinds.

Ask what the difference was between the first banana and the second. Answer: The difference is the time needed to ripen. When you find a green banana at home, you don't throw it out. Instead, you just wait and give it time to ripen.

There's a similar dynamic with believers—some are mature, some are not. Why should this be a surprise? Each of us is growing as we walk with Jesus. So, shouldn't we be patient with other people? Shouldn't we be kind, even as we want others to be patient and kind with us?

As you think through all of this, how should we view people at church?

WEEK THIRTEEN
CHURCH RELATIONSHIPS

As we wrap up our study of relationships, let's talk about people at church. Why do you go to church? Is church a building for weekend meetings? Is it like doing your devotions with other people? Is it a time to meet with friends and struggle to understand what's being taught? Is it, as some say, a club for hypocrites?

What does the Bible say about church? The New Testament uses word pictures to illustrate what the church is. The church is like a "body" (1 Corinthians 12:27), like a "temple" (Ephesians 2:19–22), and like a "flock" of sheep (1 Peter 5:1–3). Each of these terms is collective (which means a collection of parts all put together, like grapes in a bunch or players on a team).

The church is a group of Christians who have committed to regularly meet together to give and receive encouragement. This happens as they talk, listen, and help each other; as they hear God's Word taught and read; and as they work together to trust and obey God.

But is all this really necessary? What if your devotions are more helpful than church teaching? Can't you do all that church stuff on your own or with your family? Let's explore why God invented the church.

PRAYER

"Father, thank you for giving your own Son for the church. Please help me grow in understanding why the church is important. In Jesus's name. Amen."

Day 1 (GOOD)

○ Read Genesis 1:28 (below). According to this verse, what word best describes how many people God wanted on planet earth?

❏ one   ❏ several   ❏ some   ❏ a lot

> And God blessed them. And God said to them, "Be fruitful and multiply and fill the earth and subdue it, and have dominion over the fish of the sea and over the birds of the heavens and over every living thing that moves on the earth." Genesis 1:28

The Old Testament reminds us of God's original design for the human race. He never intended for people to live by themselves (Genesis 2:18a). He made us to need others; and he put together a group—a large group—of people. After all, he called his followers "my people"—there were *many* individuals united together.

God made us for himself, and he made us for relationships with other people. And in the New Testament, God created the church—the gathering together of his people.

○ List the names of five people (your age or adults) who you know and who know you at church.

○ What are three ways that other people at church can help or encourage you in your relationship with Jesus?

Day 2 (BAD)

The church is good. It's part of God's plan. But today we're going to look at the "bad news" about church. Read the following verses from 1 Corinthians. Then circle the words that describe the sin that was taking place in this church.

> For it has been reported to me by Chloe's people that there is quarreling among you, my brothers.
> 1 Corinthians 1:11
>
> It is actually reported that there is sexual immorality among you, and of a kind that is not tolerated even among pagans. 1 Corinthians 5:1a
>
> Therefore, my beloved, flee from idolatry.
> 1 Corinthians 10:14

◉ What strikes you about all this sin in this church? As you read these verses, what stood out to you?

◉ How, according to these verses, did Paul (the author of 1 Corinthians) respond to all this sin in the church? Did he think their sin and mess was no big deal?

Paul was very direct in identifying sin in this church. He gave strong commands about how members needed to repent and what they needed to change.

○ Why do you think he wrote a letter to this messed up church?

> *To help them live more like Jesus; to help them live more in harmony with the gospel of Jesus Christ.*

THINK ABOUT IT

Don't be surprised when people at church let you down, when people sin and make awful mistakes. The church, after all, is filled with sinners. When you think about it—there's no other option. We're *all* sinners. And that means the church is not a perfect place. You will be disappointed and hurt—and you may even disappoint and hurt others. But that's usually not a good reason to give up on the church. Paul didn't. God didn't. Take a moment to pray for some people in your church that may have disappointed you. Pray and ask God to help you acknowledge times when you may have disappointed others.

Day 3 (NEW)

▶ How does Jesus make "bad" church stuff "new"? Read 1 Corinthians 1:2–7 (below). Remember the verses from Day 2 of this week? For today, underline all the positive things that Paul could honestly say about the same church, the one located in Corinth.

> ² To the church of God that is in Corinth, to those sanctified in Christ Jesus, called to be saints together with all those who in every place call upon the name of our Lord Jesus Christ, both their Lord and ours: ³ Grace to you and peace from God our Father and the Lord Jesus Christ. ⁴ I give thanks to my God always for you because of the grace of God that was given you in Christ Jesus, ⁵ that in every way you were enriched in him in all speech and all knowledge— ⁶ even as the testimony about Christ was confirmed among you— ⁷ so that you are not lacking in any spiritual gift, as you wait for the revealing of our Lord Jesus Christ. 1 Corinthians 1:2–7

▶ So, according to these verses, how should you treat other Christians who don't seem to get it? How do you respond to people who seem weak or immature in their faith?

▶ What about *your* spiritual maturity? Are you working with Jesus to become more like him? Are you discouraged that it is so hard or is taking so long? As you pray about it, ask the Lord to help you take the next step toward godly change. What is that next step? Who at church can you share this with?

> Paul treated the Christians in Corinth with great kindness. Although many of the members were pretty messed up (see yesterday's devotional), Paul said encouraging things about them. He saw more of what Christ had done for them than what they themselves had been doing. In the same way, we should be patient, kind, and positive toward people who are not so mature in Christ.

IN CLOSING

TO EAT OR NOT TO EAT?

When I was in high school, sometimes church terrified me. When our church celebrated the Lord's Supper (otherwise known as the Lord's Table or Communion), our pastor would warn everyone not to eat the Lord's Supper "in an unworthy manner." He would read from 1 Corinthians 11 where Paul said that some people who had eaten "in an unworthy manner" had become sick or even died! So we were told to confess **all** our sins before participating in Communion. But what if we forgot a sin? Or what if we hadn't really confessed enough?

Then one day, years later, I realized what Paul meant about eating at the Lord's Table "in an unworthy manner." When the church in Corinth celebrated the Lord's Supper, they didn't just eat a small bit of bread and juice. The Lord's Supper was part of a church feast—a banquet. But there was a problem. Some rich people who didn't have to work would arrive early and start eating. A few hours later, when others arrived, there wasn't much food left. Just scraps. The good stuff was gone.

Some people were acting important and not thinking about other members of the church. They were not "discerning the body" (1 Corinthians 11:29). They didn't realize that there were other people who were as important in Jesus's eyes. They were *all* members of Christ's body—he died for all of them and loved all of them equally!

The Lord's Supper was a time to gather around the table as a group, a church, and a family. But the church in Corinth was celebrating this get-together feast in "an unworthy manner." This was sin.

So when your church celebrates the Lord's Supper, if your parents allow you to participate, please take time to confess your sins to the Lord. That's always right to do. But remember that the Lord is calling you to his *table*. He's inviting you to sit together as a family, *his* family. So rely on his sacrifice on the cross to cover all your sins. And then eat and enjoy being together with Christ and his body!

iStock.com/Adehoidar

WEEK THIRTEEN / CLOSING **131**

1. What stood out to you from the Word this week? (How has the Lord been using his Word to work in your life this week?)

2. Does it bother you that some people at church don't seem to "have their act together"?

3. Does it bother you that some people in church seem to always "have their act together"?

4. Do you ever look down on other people at church? Why?

5. What makes it easy to look down on people who seem different than you?

6. How should we feel about other people at church who seem to act in ways you might think of as less-than-Christian (e.g., unkind, proud, etc.)?

> **Note**: Churches include people who struggle with sin. Sometimes that sin might seem out of place in a church setting, and sometimes sin comes in the form of a religious pride that at first glance seems to fit nicely at church. For both of these types of sin, the Lord never wants us to be okay with it. As someone has said, "Jesus welcomes you just as you are, but he is never content to leave you as you are." When you are welcomed into God's family, you are given a new identity. You now belong to God (1 Corinthians 1:2). But it takes time to become who you are, to grow into godly men and women. So all of us should be patient with others and respectful of differences that God has given members of his church.

7. Should it be a goal to eventually feel that we have "arrived" in our Christian walk? What are the dangers of feeling that we have or will have one day "arrived"?

Next Steps

Help your students think about one person that they can take time to talk to after the worship service. How can they show love and patience to that person? How can they show this person that he or she is known, loved, and prayed for? Take a few minutes to plan what each of them could do, as opportunities allow, after the next church service.

Acknowledgments

I thank the Lord for the opportunity to have written this study. The perspective emphasized in *Radically Different*—using "good, bad, and new" as lenses through which to view the world—has changed *my* life. It's helped me better understand the Lord and how to live more wisely in the world he has made. I first learned about this approach in 2007, through an online sermon series by Pastor Bernard Bell, who has graciously given permission to use his good, bad, and new categories for this study.

Additionally, this study wouldn't exist without the efforts of many people. Several have been extremely helpful discussion partners through the writing process: Dr. Bruce Ashford, Dr. Roger Erdvig, Dr. Blake Hardcastle, Dr. Curtis Hill, Rev. Chris Morris, and Dr. Bryan Smith. I'm grateful for the support and encouragement of New Growth Press: the leadership of Karen Teears, the guidance of Barbara Juliani, and the insights of Nancy Winter and the rest of the editorial team. I'm also thrilled to once again team up with illustrator Scot McDonald, whose design makes written words so much more fun to read.

Finally, a word of appreciation for my son, Micah, to whom this book is dedicated. He gave up part of his summer break to read Dad's book and provided great feedback. I pray this book encourages him and every reader toward the Lord and all his ways.

Notes

1. From the title of a book by Craig G. Bartholomew and Michael W. Goheen, *The True Story of the Whole World: Finding Your Place in the Biblical Drama* (Grand Rapids: Faith Alive Christian Resources, 2004).

2. Though the general concepts were not unfamiliar, the terminology of "good/bad/new" was first presented to me through the teaching ministry of Pastor Bernard Bell at Peninsula Bible Church Cupertino. Used by permission.

3. Michael Williams, in Dane Ortlund, "What's the Message of the Bible in One Sentence," Strawberry-Rhubarb Thelogy, January 12, 2011, http://dogmadoxa.blogspot.com/2011/01/whats-message-of-bible-in-one-sentence.html.

4. C. S. Lewis, *Mere Christianity* (New York: HarperOne, 1952), 175–76.

5. Adapted from George Herbert, "The Elixir" in George Herbert, *The Complete English Works*, ed. Ann Pasternak Slater, in Everyman's Library (New York: Alfred A. Knopf, 1995), 180.

6. The concepts of "structure" and "direction" are taken from Albert M. Wolters, *Creation Regained: Biblical Basics for a Reformational Worldview*, 2nd ed. (Grand Rapids: Eerdmans, 2005), 87–89.

7. Adapted from Bruce Ashford and Chris Pappalardo, *One Nation Under God: A Christian Hope for American Politics* (Nashville: B & H Publishing Group, 2015), 16.

8. These contrasting phrases adapted from Ashford and Pappalardo, *One Nation Under God*, 16.

9. Adapted from John Piper, "The Worship of the Christian Leader," November 8, 1991, transcript and audio, https://www.desiringgod.org/messages/the-worship-of-the-christian-leader.

10. Adapted from Michael Oh, "Honor Thy Father and Mother," lecture, CROSS Conference, December 29, 2013, audio, http://crossforthenations.org/media/2014/01/honor-thy-father-and-mother/. Used by permission.

11. Daniel James Brown, *The Boys in the Boat: Nine Americans and Their Epic Quest for Gold at the 1936 Berlin Olympics* (New York: Viking, 2013), 234–35, 249.

12. Adapted from Ken Sande, "Staying on Top of Conflict," Relational Wisdom 360, accessed August 2018, https://rw360.org/slippery-slope/.

13. Rachel Lewis, "Suicide Rate for Teen Girls Hits 40-Year High," *Time*, August 4, 2017, http://time.com/4887282/teen-suicide-rate-cdc.